(continued from front flap)

patience, an ability to follow instructions, and a desire to restore the beauty of a valued antique. Everything that can be done at home to give a new lease on life to a treasured antique is carefully described in this book. Materials are recommended, suppliers are listed, and step-by-step processes are outlined for the treatment of furniture, paintings, books, glass, silver, carpets, and many other items.

To complete the link between antiques and the home, there are suggestions for adapting, using, and displaying restored articles.

Refurbishing Antiques provides information that will save the reader time and money. Mrs. Ratcliff's instructions will spare the antiques owner the lengthy search for a professional, the costly consultant's fee, and the frustration of not knowing how to treat a specific item. Most importantly, the owner will know the satisfaction of refurbishing and beautifying a beloved antique.

REFURBISHING ANTIQUES

REFURBISHING

Illustrated by Ted Western

ANTIQUES

Rosemary Ratcliff

HENRY REGNERY COMPANY
Chicago

Contents

Acknowledgments

I am very grateful to all the people who helped —I could not have produced this book without them.

In particular I would like to thank Messrs. Tracy, Hill, Daborn, Sielle, Bray, Fenton, Usher, Manus, Woodhatch, Simpkin, Appleby, Barker, Webb, Behar, Wolff, Diamond; Mrs. Hunter; and Miss Thorold.

Introduction

Restoration is an emotive subject and one that experts will always disagree about. A lot of people, for a start, are not always clear what they mean when they talk about restoring. As one cabinet maker said, "Do they mean the piece should look as it might have been when it was first made, or as it would be now three hundred years later if it had been treated well all that time?"

If owners of damaged goods can have different aims, so can restorers. One might love the feeling that a broken piece is being given a new lease on life and tend it back to working order as a doctor looks after a patient; another might simply want to deceive in order to make money.

Restorers and those seeking professional help are caught in a vicious circle. Craftsmen face such escalating costs that the work they can take on is becoming limited; it takes the same amount of time to mend an Edwardian or a Sheraton desk, but if the cost is going to be more than $100, it may be more than the Edwardian one is worth—so the Sheraton, which is valuable enough to stand the cost, is taken on, while the Edwardian is abandoned to its fate. Few youngsters these days will withstand the long apprenticeship and small returns that the old one-man repairer was willing to undergo; one elderly craftsman, referring to a colleague of his who was still working at eighty, said, "What can we do? We have no pension, only our skill."

I hope this book will provide one small break in the vicious circle of abandoning old goods and paying exorbitant prices for new and help owners return their old, valued, or simply treasured possessions back into use. You will find at the end of the book a list of the people who were kind enough to help me in compiling it.

REFURBISHING ANTIQUES

1 Furniture and Wood

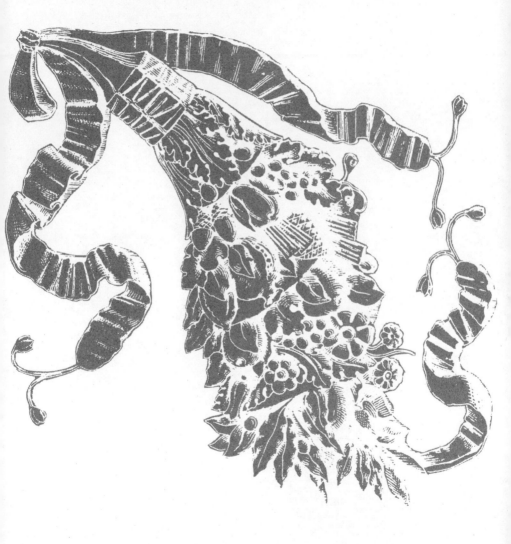

Wood, however long since it was part of a tree, is still living matter. It will still swell in the wet, shrink in the dry, and provide food for insects. This is because, although the cell walls have dried out, the cell matter is still there; the wood is really like a hard sponge. This means that, whenever it has been abused by climate, people, or insects, the damage is to a certain extent reversible.

Wood finish—stain and polish—has two purposes: to put a protective layer between the open pores and the outside elements and to bring out the patterns and textures which are the essence of wood's appeal. It can be something of a shock to see a piece of, say, mahogany before treatment—it's flat and thoroughly dull. But just a touch of stain makes it spring to life. The appeal of wood furniture is surely unlimited; in an increasingly standardized world it's a nice thought that the tree that provided the wood for your dining room table was quite unique and that no other grew to make just those patterns.

Generally speaking, the hardest woods come from tropical

climates and the softest from the most northern. The following are the principal woods, with their origins and characteristics.

Softwoods
Pine

The usual pine used for furniture is the soft white variety of the northern states, although the harder Southern pine is sometimes encountered.

European Spruce

Known as whitewood and used for cheap furniture.

Yew

An irregular grower, giving uneven rings. It's a very tough wood, almost as strong as oak.

Hardwoods
Amboyna

A rich, light brown wood, with small bird's eye patterns, it comes from the West Indies.

African Walnut

A lighter variety than the American.

Aformosia

From Africa, it looks a bit like teak.

Beech

Usually used for chairs, due to its strength (tougher than oak) ; it's prone to worm, though.

Boxwood

A yellow, heavy wood without any patterning.

Ebony

A very hard wood, comes from either Africa or India.

Elm

An irregular, cross-grained wood.

Kingwood

It is like rosewood, but it is lighter in color and comes from Brazil.

Lignumvitae

This is one of the hardest and heaviest of woods (about three or four times as hard as English oak, for example) ; it comes from Central and South America and the West Indies.

Mahogany, African

The pores are larger than those of the American variety, giving it a coarser look; the color is lighter and the patterns come in a wide variety.

Mahogany, American

The names for this cause some confusion; Spanish mahogany is desirable for furniture, but it doesn't mean the wood comes from Spain. It is often from the West Indies or the adjacent mainland, which was under Spanish control in the 1700s when the wood became popular. It is close-grained, with a silky texture and a natural luster. The best mahogany of all comes from Cuba. There is also a variety from America proper, which is straight-grained with a compact texture.

Maple

Curly and Bird's Eye are the two main varieties, coming generally from North America (the sap goes to make maple syrup) .

Cherry

Stronger than oak.

Oak

An odd wood—because it is acid and contains tannin, which acts as a built-in preservative—it can be left untreated and would last. The acid causes the wood to corrode lead, and the tannin will cause stains if the wood is in contact with iron or iron compounds.

Poplar

A wood that probably makes its appearance more than people realize—it can be made to simulate maple, mahogany, walnut, or rosewood.

Rosewood

Comes from Honduras or India, more often the latter country; the Madagascan variety looks like tulipwood.

Sapele

A variety of mahogany found in Africa, harder and heavier than the others.

Satinwood

Comes from India, Ceylon, or the West Indies.

Teak

A wood that is long-lasting and strong for its weight; comes from the Far East.

Tulipwood

A yellowish brown with reddish stripes, it comes from Brazil.

Walnut

There are two varieties, American and European, but the latter is most widely used (particularly that from France or Italy) . The richly patterned veneers so popular on furniture come from only a small number of trees, and then only from a small part of the tree—the stump, burr, and crotch.

From tree to dining room table involves a number of processes. After the wood is cut, it has to be dried thoroughly. In the past this meant drying in the air, which was long and hazardous, but nowadays steam drying is the usual process. The bark has more moisture than the heart and so takes longer. Then the log has to be cut into usable pieces. This can be done lengthwise, crosswise, on the bias, or round

Loo Table

and round like peeling an apple. The way the wood is cut determines the pattern the finished wood will show; large pored woods especially can look very different according to the ways they are cut. Up to about 1830 the cutting could only be done on a long saw, but the introduction of the rotary saw speeded up the process (this is a very useful guide for telling the age of furniture, as it is not difficult to tell if a straight or rotary saw has been used). The peeling method is quite modern and is used mainly for plywood.

The selection of wood for veneers is an art in itself, needing an artistic eye that can envision the plank as a made-up piece. Technically, any wood can be stained any color, but the traditional stains emphasize the natural color already present. After the wood is stained, the pores are filled with a plaster composition, and the whole is polished, which both seals the wood and acts as a refractory layer to give the patterns even more depth.

Imagine an oak dresser made about 1700 in Shropshire. It was a sturdy piece, constructed for a large, bleak farmhouse, the only furniture of any importance apart from the bed.

The couple who bought it new from the local cabinet maker were young, and the wife proudly polished it with beeswax once a day. But gradually it lost its pristine look as cats climbed over it, dogs chewed the legs, water was spilled on it, mud and dirt from the farm swept over it—and each week the beeswax ground the marks and dirt in further.

The front of the dresser was darkened by smoke from the open fire, while sunshine bleached the far end. Dampness from the floor seeped up into the legs, only to be dried out in summer; the wood was continually contracting and expanding until eventually the legs warped so much that the dresser no longer stood straight.

When the couple died, their son inherited the farmhouse, but he never married; and at his death the dresser was moved to his niece's farm, some ten miles away. Laboriously, it was loaded on to a cart and jolted over the trail. One of the stretchers worked loose, a couple of drawers fell out, and a knob disappeared from the top.

The niece was houseproud and slowly built up a shine again with beeswax. The stretcher was secured with a wooden pin, a new leg cut for the warped one. But one drawer continued to stick, and woodworm found its way into one of the juicy, damp legs.

When the niece died, her children had left Shropshire for the Midlands, where the industrial revolution was promising rich rewards. So the farmhouse was sold and the dresser turned out into the yard, where it was a handy surface for mixing chicken feed on. One day a passing tinker spotted it and offered the farmer sixty cents for it, which was accepted.

The dresser was pulled into two pieces, loaded onto the barrow, and driven into Birmingham's Bull Ring on market day. There the housekeeper of a newly prosperous young couple spotted it and realized it would come in very useful in her new kitchen. She gave the tinker ninety cents for it, had it taken home, dried it out, and covered it in several layers of solid, serviceable brown paint. The sticking drawer was replaced by a new one.

The next generation had the kitchen redecorated, and the dresser collected a covering of cream-colored paint. It wasn't until the next generation that the dresser was given a chance to shine again. We're up to date now, and the couple are madly keen on antiques, furnishing their house as cheaply as possible with the old and beautiful. When grandmother dies they scour her house, realize the age of the dresser, and with loving care start clearing off 250 years of neglect.

The point this story illustrates is that every piece of furniture has been used and virtually every piece has at some time or other been out of fashion. We tend to forget that dining tables have continuously been eaten from, chairs have been sat in millions of times, desks have seen reams of letters written. To think that in the 1900s they used to break up Regency furniture for firewood!

In fact, every piece of furniture acts as a diary, recording events. That white round stain was where Aunt Milly put a wet vase of flowers down in 1921; that spot where the French polish has come away originated from Uncle George's drunken revelry in 1918 when a bottle of port was knocked over.

And even if furniture avoids stains, there's plenty of less direct damage it can suffer. Warping can be caused by extremes in temperature or, worse, extremes of humidity; a hard, dry winter can be dangerous, and of course the dry atmosphere of central heating can be lethal. Wood shrinks more in its width than in its length, so veneers can rise or split if at variance with the layer underneath (and damp can loosen the glues, causing the veneer to come adrift.)

Backs are often made of cheaper, softer wood, and it's here, where it's dark and dirty, that worms move in to wreak their havoc unseen until holes announce their departure.

Stress can affect all joints. Just moving furniture to clean underneath its puts strain on the legs, and a chair is a finely balanced piece of ergonomics, which easily becomes unbalanced if only one part, say an arm, is broken. And of course there are never-ending dents and scratches to add to their deterioration. No wonder furniture dealers say that virtually every piece they handle has to have some work done on it. But nothing is so awful that it can't be remedied.

Polishing

Imagine first of all a miracle—a piece of furniture that has been cared for all through its life, that has nothing broken or missing, and its age shows only in one way: through a lovely rich patina of polished wood. This patina will not only be pleasing, it will also add enormously to the value of the piece because original patina in good condition is very rare.

All that it needs now is careful maintenance. Most women would leap in with the wax polish and with each hard push of the elbow imagine that they were doing something called "feeding the wood." This, in fact, is nonsense. If the piece has been well finished, there shouldn't be any "wood" to feed—it should be well sealed with shellac.

All that women do with wax polishing is to satisfy some

primitive houseproud instinct; the wood, in fact, could even be adversely affected. If the cloth picks up a bit of grit, the surface will be scratched; if dust is not carefully wiped from the table first, it will simply be ground in with the wax; and if the wax is too pale, it will leave a white smear.

The ideal daily care for French polish is a daily wipe over with soap and lukewarm water and a yearly wax polish (and the accumulated wax polish ought to be taken off after five years with mineral spirits).

However, if the piece of furniture is not sophisticated—a Victorian pembroke table, for instance—and the surface is dull, then wax polish is very useful for building up a shine that is softer and less new looking than a French polish. Wax polish is really only a general term; the waxes and ingredients that make up a brand-name polish can vary enormously. The basic mixture is half paraffin wax and half beeswax, with a hard wax such as carnauba added in. But women prefer their work easier today, so the hard wax is usually left out and mineral spirits, which softens the mixture and makes it easier to apply, is added instead. The special "antique" waxes probably still have some hard wax in them, but if you really want to build up a shine, use Simoniz car wax, which is very hard. Shoe polish, incidentally, is simply colored wax and can be useful if furniture and polish colors match exactly.

If the surface is not just dull, but generally worn, with dirt, stains, and small scratches, and you don't want to have it French polished, try a "reviver" mixture. Formulas for these are legion, but they all have their possibilities. Try any of these:

(1) 1 qt. warm water, 3 tbs. boiled linseed oil, 1 tbs. turpentine

(2) 2 tbs. linseed oil, 1 tbs. turpentine, 5 tbs. alcohol

(3) ½ pt. each linseed oil, turpentine, vinegar; small tsp. alcohol

(4) 1 pt. raw linseed oil, 1 pt. vinegar.

Apply, then build up the surface again with wax polish.

Unfortunately, the surface usually has specific blemishes, and the problem is to know which can be tackled at home and which need specialized treatment. One cabinet maker, when I asked him what an amateur could safely do, said "as in the case of marriage, don't"—he had suffered too much from having to rescue botched attempts at home restoration.

However, I think this is too harsh. Provided the amateur knows the hazards and allows for paying a professional if the job should prove too difficult, then there is a reasonable amount he can do at home. Find out the value of the piece first, just in case it's more than you thought.

Scratches

Scratches pose the most common problem. Rescue depends partly on the depth of the scratch and partly on how perfect you want the surface to be.

If the scratches are not too deep, the simplest way is to fill them with continuous applications of colored wax (mix umber into ordinary household wax polish to get the right color). This will gradually bring them up to the level of the rest of the surface.

A more complicated way is to fill the scratches in with French polish (this is assuming they don't go into the stain and wood). Rub along the scratch gently with fine sandpaper or wire wool to make a curved pit instead of a deep-sided gorge. Then paint in the French polish with a fine paintbrush (check the chart on page 29 for the right variety of polish). When each layer has dried, which will be in about half an hour if it is thin, rub down again with fine sandpaper, and paint on another layer. Don't worry about rubbing a bit of the surrounding polish each time, and don't worry about the patch looking worse than it was. It will appear very dull each time you rub down. Once the area is level and has a gentle smoothing off, a wax polish will soon merge it into its surroundings. The spot will probably look duller than the rest of the surface for a while, but it will be less noticeable than the scratch.

If the scratch has gone through the polish into the stain, the operation is going to be much more complicated. Reapplying the stain means matching the color, which in turn means a lot of mixing and pondering. Try rubbing down to the wood on a part of the furniture that doesn't show and testing possible stains on it. When you feel confident of the color, brush it on in the direction of the grain, leave it 24 hours to dry, then apply the French polish as before.

Fine scratches in French polish can also be eliminated by applying alcohol, which melts the polish and lets it flow together again. It sounds fine in theory, but in practice I have found that the surface becomes soft, tacky, and rather unmanageable, and the mark becomes worse than before.

Removing Dents and Filling Holes

Removing dents is something that sounds complicated but is in fact not too difficult. Remember the analogy about wood being like a hard sponge; a dent is simply cells squashed together, and if they are allowed to soak up moisture, they can swell back to shape again.

Take off any wax with turpentine, put a pad of wet blotting paper over the dent and keep it wet for several hours. Remove the blotting paper and put a bottle cap, rim side up, on the dent; rest an iron at its lowest heat on it. Look every five minutes or so to see if the dent is filling out; it may not come entirely smooth, but at least it will be better than it was before.

If the wood is very close grained, make tiny pin pricks in the dent to allow steam to enter. Do this anyway if the dent proves obstinate.

If there is a definite hole, rather than a dent, it is perfectly easy to fill but is likely to be rather noticeable if you do it yourself; if it is in a spot where it matters, take the piece to a professional. Otherwise, try it yourself.

There are three possible brands of fillers; beaumontage, brummer stopping, and plastic wood. Beaumontage is a mixture of resin, beeswax and shellac and is the most established material still used by most professionals. However, it is quite difficult to handle and, as it will not take stain, needs to be color-matched very carefully.

Beaumontage looks like sealing wax and behaves the same way; hold it over the hole, apply a soldering iron, and let it drip into the hole. The surface is then smoothed down with sandpaper. The problem is to drop just enough in not to have to do a vast rubbing down of the remainder (if you're rubbing fiercely, you're likely to harm the surrounding wood). You may have to enlarge a small hole or the filler will have a tendency to drop out. The bottom of the hole should always be scored to ensure a firm hold.

Brummer stopping seems to be used a lot by the lower end of the cabinet trade, as it is easy to mold, but I have found it difficult to use and not entirely satisfactory. The problem is staining it to the right color; apparently this has to be done before it is fully dry, but the colors are strong anyway, and there seems to be a temptation to use it as it is. I had an oval Victorian dining-table done up by a cheap polisher once, and all the dents were filled with a dark brummer stopping that looked awful against the lighter surface. Also, it comes out quite smooth, with no "wood" texture, so it tends to show up as a filler even if the color match is good.

Finally, there's plastic wood, which I think is a splendid invention, capable of merging almost completely into natural wood. After a certain amount of experiment, I have found walnut the best all-purpose shade; it's a mid-brown, which takes stains well and seems to make an equally good mahogany, rosewood, or oak. The natural color is useful for light colored oak, while the mahogany I found is like brummer stopping—too smooth and also a very strong red.

Score the hole at the bottom to help the plastic wood hold (although if you're filling in an edge piece or a long strip, it's sometimes best to shape the plastic wood, detach it, and stick it back with Araldite, which prevents it being caught and pulled off later). Fill in gradually, letting each layer of plastic wood dry well, and push it well down. One of the secrets of success is a very smooth surface.

Take as much time as possible rubbing down—any pits or ridges will show up far more after staining. Work down to a very fine sandpaper, so that you can run your finger along the whole surface and not feel where the filler is. Plastic wood shrinks a bit as it dries, so don't make the final judgment until you are sure it has finished shrinking.

The great advantage of plastic wood is that it takes a stain very well, so that you can end up with an almost invisible patch. Stains are labeled according to the woods they resemble, not the woods they have to be used on. For example, a dark oak can be used on mahogany and vice versa, while walnut is again a very useful color on a variety of woods. For a long time I didn't realize this, and I suffered agonies if I dabbed "oak" stain onto a piece of walnut, wondering what damage I had done. I think manufacturers could make the usage clearer.

Anyway, you can mix the stains quite freely to get the right color, remembering that they will dry lighter. If the match is not successful, I find that it's often possible to use a darker color and merge it into the surrounding wood so that it looks like a darker or dirtier patch. Rub down a certain amount of the surrounding wood as well, apply the stain, and, if you can bear the mess, use a finger to smudge the edges in. Use increasingly darker stain and rub in smaller and smaller circles, so that the patch in the middle is completely invisible, but its darkness is merged in. The plastic wood soaks up quite a bit of stain, so let it dry out well before judging the final effect.

Finish with French polish as described on page 28. If the

patch still looks noticeable after the first layer of French polish, I simply brush another layer of stain on top, which is strictly against the rules but seems to work.

If the hole to be filled is small, use the professional's mixture of sawdust and glue, which can make the most invisible repair of all.

Woodworm Holes

Woodworm holes are a separate problem, because any filler tends to sink down into the network of tunnels. Moreover, worms have a nasty habit of making themselves a labyrinth inside the wood, with only a few exit holes to reveal their presence. So be careful when you rub around a hole, or you may find the piece disintegrating. When cabinet makers know a honeycomb like this exists, they strengthen it by pouring in liquid glue; amateurs, I think, should hand this problem over to professionals rather than try this themselves (it's sometimes easier to make a completely new part anyway).

Cigarette Burns

A cigarette burn is probably the worst disaster, because you can't see how far down the wood has charred. You start to sandpaper it away and realize that you're about an inch below the surface of the wood and about to come out the other side. So tackle it gently. Rub away the loose charred wood and try a bleach (an ordinary household variety will do). Or it might be possible to mask the spot by painting on a darker stain and merging it into the surrounding wood (see page 12). Otherwise it's a matter of laboriously filling in the hole.

Marks on Wood

Marks on the wood shouldn't be a problem, because the French polish should prevent their soaking into the wood and leaving a stain. However, there can be something in the substance that acts as a catalyst and dissolves the polish, allowing the stain to go through.

Alcohol is the worst in this respect, so leave plenty of coasters around if you're holding a party in a room with French polished furniture in it. If the mark is not too bad, you might be able to merge the polish back again. Drop a small amount of linseed oil onto a clean cloth and stroke the mark gently. Or it might come off with a very fine sandpaper (polish well afterwards).

However, you are more likely to find that you have to rub the half-dissolved polish right off and fill up the patch with fresh French polish (see page 28). If the mark is in the shape of a ring, you will get better results if you rub down the middle as well, leaving a complete round piece to be filled in (but always brush both stain and polish in the direction of the grain, not around in circles.

Ink stains can be removed by rubbing them with weak nitric acid (about 5%—your local druggist might make you up a small amount of solution). The mark will probably go slightly white, but a rub with a cloth will take this away. A weak solution of sodium hypochlorite mixed with vinegar is also very effective. Dab a little vinegar onto the stain with a soft brush, and dab the 10% solution of sodium hypochlorite onto this. The ink will gradually be bleached away. Try not to remove all the stain with one application, as it is easy to overdo the bleaching effect and attack the wood. Finally, rinse off and repolish.

White heat marks might require major repair but sometimes can be removed simply. Mix an equal amount of linseed oil and turpentine, leave it to soak on the mark for several hours, and remove with vinegar.

Water marks are fairly common, leaving a white stain caused by the water's condensation and slow evaporation. The method of elimination depends on how far the mark has penetrated. If it is only slight, you might remove it by rubbing with Brasso. If this doesn't work, rub with the finest steel wool and oil (this is advantageous because the steel wool is polishing the layer underneath as well as removing the stain).

If the water has penetrated through the polish to the wood, the repair is much more complicated. The wood will have turned black and will need bleaching, which is really a professional job. However, this is the recipe for removing the mark: make a saturate solution of oxalic acid crystals in a pint of water (that is, mix until no more crystals will dissolve), brush on, and rinse well with plain water.

When the spot has dried out, it will need building up again with stain and French polish (see pages 27 and 28). To prevent water spots it is a good idea to put a mat under anything containing water; even if you wipe the bottom of a container, there may be a crack you haven't noticed.

Furniture Repairs

The first requirements for doing major furniture repairs are space and a good light; this I have learned from bitter experience, after trying to do a certain amount of mending in a small, dark flat. However, given these and a practical turn of mind, you can do quite a lot at home.

Chairs get broken probably more than any other piece of furniture, as they are subject to the most stress. I have referred before to the ergonomics of a chair; what I mean is that the pressure is not just on the four legs as you would imagine, but it is spread in a delicate balance between the legs, back, and arms. So you should never ignore a broken arm because it is never rested on; even without pressure, a broken arm will throw the whole chair out of alignment and possibly cause something else to break.

Joints

In the same way, there is a definite balance of firm and floating joints, and if this is upset, there is danger of a break. All arms and rungs should be securely fixed and reglued as soon as they show signs of loosening. But the slats at the back should move freely; if they are fixed, again the whole chair is subject to strain.

When doing any repair on a chair, have a look at the joints and adjust any that are wrong so that you can avoid later trouble. Sometimes a part of the joint may have worn down too far to be simply reglued. The gap can be filled up with matchsticks without adjusting the other joints, but this is not always entirely satisfactory. The alternative is to take the whole chair apart and build it up again.

This is a somewhat alarming procedure and not to be recommended for best Regency or Sheraton chairs. Tie layers of cloth around a hammer head and knock the chair at key points. Then build the chair up again slowly, using splinters or toothpicks to fill in gaps (an assistant is helpful to hold pieces while you're judging the correct angle of the new joint).

Screws should never be used on furniture, not only for aesthetic but also for practical reasons; they hold a joint too rigidly so that too much strain is put on other joints. If there are any screws in the furniture you are dismantling, they may prove difficult to remove, having rusted in. Try applying a red hot poker, if you have one, or heat up a metal implement in a gas jet. If that doesn't work, nick across the wood on either side so that you can grip the wood with pliers. And if you are going to replace the screws, grease them first with candle wax.

Glue is the only adhesive that should ever be used, and generally it should only be Scotch or animal glue, which is difficult to use. This is made from boiled bones or skin and has good elasticity, which allows the joint to give slightly. It has to be mixed (never boiled or heated directly over a naked flame), applied in a warm atmosphere, and left for some time to dry. It is not heat- or water-proof, and insects like it. But all the good cabinet makers say you should use no other.

The only exception is inlay work; then a cellulose-based glue such as Durofix is best.

Scotch glue comes in either a powder or a solid form; it is heated in a special glue pot, but never over a naked flame as it is inflammable. When it's runny, it's ready. The work must be done in a warm atmosphere; otherwise, the glue goes through some drastic chemical change and disintegrates. Because of the long period of drying (about 8 hours), clamps are necessary for awkward joints. Here the amateur needs ingenuity, since his range of clamps is likely to be limited. Tourniquets can often be useful; stick bits of wood in the joint as hard as they will go. (See Fig. 1.)

The American restorer B. Grotz has a very neat system for holding flat pieces of wood together while they are sticking. The first step is to hammer nails round them on the floor. He assumes that you have floor handy that you can hammer into. You lay the two pieces on the floor and put the nails in either side to hold them together as tightly as possible. (See Fig. 2.)

Warped Wood

I am also indebted to B. Grotz for a method of taking the warp out of wood. Warp is caused by the contracting of one side of the wood through heat or the expansion of the other through damp. To cure it, one must reverse the process. Lay the piece, says Mr. Grotz, hump side up on the grass, and put a heavy rock on top. Then you simply let nature take its

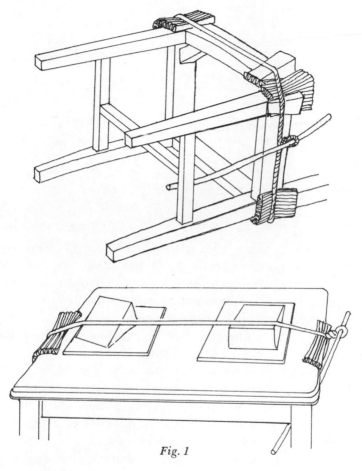

Fig. 1

course. The wet grass will swell out one side, the sun will dry up the other and, presto, you'll end up with a flat plank.

That is the principle for repairing warps, although it is possible to do it more gently by laying wet sawdust on the inside of the curve or by laying the hump side, if the piece

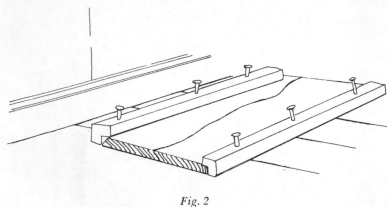

Fig. 2

is not too large, on a stove with jets off and the oven on. If wetting the wood makes it curve the other way, this will probably be corrected when it dries. However, cabinet makers often find it not worth the time to fiddle around with any cure; it may quicker to cut a new piece.

If a piece of furniture has been warped as a result of flooding, and you can bear to look at the warp for a considerable time, it may be possible to let nature slowly straighten things out. I had a wooden box that stood in a few inches of water for about sixteen hours and was considerably shrunken and out of shape. In disgust I flung it to the back of a closet, but this year, some three and a half years after the accident, I found it again—returned to perfect shape. So don't collapse in total despair when faced with water-damaged furniture.

Broken Joints

Broken joints in vulnerable positions will have to be held together by a dowel as well as glue (see Fig. 3). These breaks are likely to be on chairs and most likely to be on legs, where a curved piece of wood has a very short grain withstanding a lot of stress.

Dowelling pins can be bought in packs; it is important to realize that the measurements on the pins refer to their size *before* they have been smoothed down, and they are actually slightly smaller than they say. In other words, if you use a ¼-in. bit to bore a hole for a ¼-in. dowelling pin, the hole will be slightly too large—and a tight fit is very important for the operation. So use a bit that is slightly smaller than the dowel.

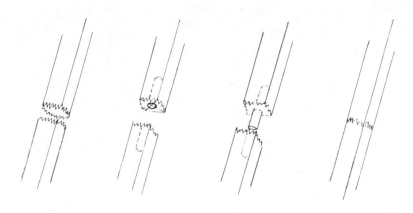

Fig. 3

To find the center point in which to drill, draw diagonal lines from opposite corners; where they intersect is the right spot to drill. If there is another weak spot either above or below the break, take the pin through it to prevent another breakage later. The dowel should always go at right angles to the line of breakage, regardless of the shape of the piece being mended.

Some breaks can be strengthened by means of wedges and struts at the top of chair legs (see Fig. 4). Sometimes it's

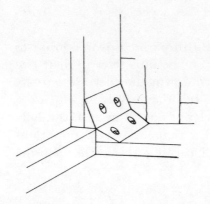

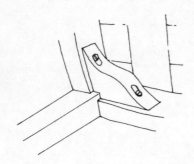

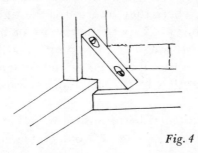

Fig. 4

even possible to incorporate them into the design of the chair. (See Fig. 5.)

If a broken end is stuck in a hole, there is a comparatively simple way to remove it. Bore a hole dead center through the broken part, surround the area with a cloth wrung out in boiling water to melt any glue, twist a screw into the hole, and pull the whole piece out with a pair of pincers gripped around the screw.

One small hint for swivel top tables—if the top has become loose, it's sometimes possible to renew it by switching the top around.

Removing Polish

French polishing has whole books devoted to it, full of complicated looking charts and processes which seem

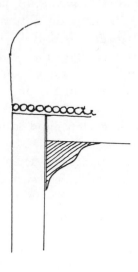

Fig. 5

fraught with difficulty. Certainly, to do it really well and in large areas, it is a very skilled job. But to *use* French polish with moderate success it not too difficult, and it's the most satisfying of restoring processes.

How much you remove of the old polish and stain depends on the state of the surface of the furniture and the kind of new surface you want. Personally, I don't like furniture of any age to look too gleaming and would prefer a few blemishes to a clean, highly polished dazzle (as restorer Mr. Watts said, "I like a piece to have a bit of distress").

If you're stripping the piece right down, it is easiest to use a patent paint stripper. Otherwise alcohol and fine wire wool remove the polish. Then you sandpaper the stain. The object is to remove the layers as effortlessly as possible and to scuff up the wood as little as possible. In other words, you could take it off more quickly with a coarse sandpaper, but it will take a long time to smooth the wood down again.

At all stages of the work, it is vital to have a good light (a really good restorer will insist on natural overhead light). At this point, for instance, it is only by looking at the surface sideways under a strong light that you can see that there are no sandpaper or wire wool tracks; since stain and polish will magnify such unnatural marks, it is very important to see they have all disappeared. It's a shame, though, to take out all the natural looking dents and squiggles—they're part of the antique "distress."

If the wood is open grained (for example, oak), dampen it before doing the final rubbing down. This will raise the grain that might otherwise be brought up by the staining. It is always useful to wrap sandpaper around a wood block, since this prevents a small indentation from becoming large.

There are three main types of stain. The difference is in the base liquid in which the color is distilled—either water, spirit, or oil.

Staining

Water stain is the oldest variety, still regularly used by the trade now, who think it's the best, despite the fact that it raises the grain of the wood slightly; it has a good color, and it spreads and penetrates well.

Spirit stain is the one most widely sold in shops under brand names. It penetrates as well as water stain and has the advantage of not raising the grain; but it dries rapidly (the speed of drying increases with heat), so you must take care that the edges don't overlap, or there is a likelihood of streaks. It also has a tendency to fade over a period of time.

Oil stain is not as penetrating as the other two; since it is likely to have the same medium as wax polish, the color may come off later with polishing, unless it is well sealed in.

When staining, remember that grain running horizontally looks lighter than grain running vertically, so you may have to adjust the shade on some pieces (look at the pieces *in situ* to judge best). End grain absorbs more stain than the ordinary top grain, so cover it with a layer or so of French polish before staining, or it will turn out darker.

As I have said before, the names on the stains, for example, mahogany, walnut, oak, do not mean they have to be used exclusively on those woods—they just mean "mahogany color," "walnut color," and so on.

If you are in doubt about the shade, start light by diluting the stain with either water or spirit, according to the variety, and build up with several layers.

It's certainly a lovely moment when you first brush the stain on—the wood seems to spring to life. Use straight strokes along the grain, and be careful not to overlap; within a few minutes, when the surface has dried, polish with a cloth. This will remove a certain amount of unevenness.

Leave it to dry properly for about a day before moving on to the next stage.

The grain now has a great many open pores, which need to be filled in to give a really smooth surface. Here the amateurs and professionals part company. I confess that I simply paint on two or three layers of French polish, which is very much the quick and easy method (but allowable).

The thorough way is to use a powdery filler—either superfine plaster of paris or a brand name filler that has·a base of china clay or writing and is already colored.

To apply plaster of paris, dip a damp cloth into the dry plaster and rub a small area of the work in a circular motion —since the plaster dries rapidly, the whole thing has to be done quickly. Before the plaster has dried, rub it with a coarse sacking. When the plaster is thoroughly dry (looking alarmingly white), wipe on linseed oil to "kill" the plaster. Then rub well with a garnet paper, which will make a goo of the oil and plaster, and wipe off the surplus with a rag.

It is possible to mix vandyke brown powder into the plaster first to color it, but a proprietary brand is much easier to use; all you have to do is thin it with turpentine, rub it across the grain with a coarse cloth, and rub off the surplus with a rag. It comes in all the usual wood colors.

French Polishing

French polishing can be used either for a quick renovation or for a completely new surface. I have never tackled anything larger than a small desk, and even quite poor surfaces have turned out quite well with the quick method. Sandpaper out as many of the scratches and marks as you want to, always taking care that harsh sandpaper tracks are not left (look along the surface sideways in a good light). Leave as much or as little of the original French polish as you choose. Technically, it is wiser to apply a layer of varnish with a rubber (see page 33 and Fig. 9) to separate the old and new polishes, because the spirit in the new polish might partially dissolve the old (but I have never seen this happen). Then brush on several layers of French polish, rubbing each one down with fine wire wool. The last few layers can be wiped on with a linen cloth, and at the end a small amount of rottenstone powder applied gently on a cloth will cut down unevenness and give a very good shine. Finish off with several layers of wax polish to give a natural look.

Occasionally, on a nice rich piece of mahogany, I have tried the proper "fadding" with linseed oil and a fad, but the only result was to reinforce my respect for professional French polishers. The technique is obviously something that needs a lot of practice, so here, for diligent amateur restorers, are the details.

The polish itself is made from shellac, which is extracted by parasitic insects from banyan trees in India; it dissolves in alcohol and dries hard as the alcohol evaporates. There are four shades—button, white, garnet, and orange, which represent four different kinds of shellac dissolved in methylated spirits.

Button is used mainly on oak and unstained or golden walnut; it tends to cloud mahogany.

White is for unstained or very light woods.

Garnet is a rich greenish-brown and is used over dark colors—dark walnut, mahogany, or ordinary oak.

Orange is for golden colors and the variety most frequently found in hardware stores.

The stages of the process make it sound like an undertaker's laying out—fadding, bodying, and stiffing. Joking aside, though, each one is vitally important and cannot be skimped.

First you will need a specially prepared "fad"; fold a piece of unbleached wadding into a pear shape, soak it in polish, leave it to dry out, and dip it into alcohol before using (this prevents hairs from sticking to the work). (See Fig. 6.)

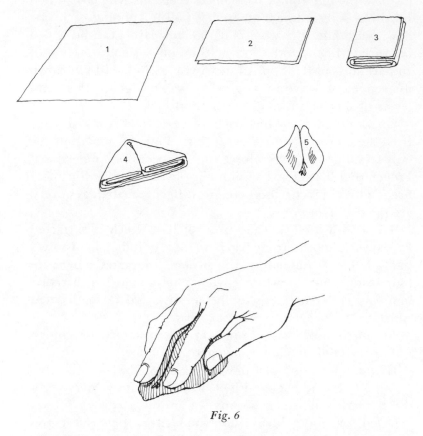

Fig. 6

With the fad, work the polish backward and forward along the grain, going over each layer afterward with fine sand-paper. Do about three layers; this will fill up any open pores. Then spread some drops of boiled linseed oil over the work, soak the fad in polish, and use the classical movements to spread it over the work: first make small circles all over to lay a good foundation (see Fig. 7); next make figure eights in the middle and circular movements round the edges (see Fig. 8); then form long figure eights the whole length of

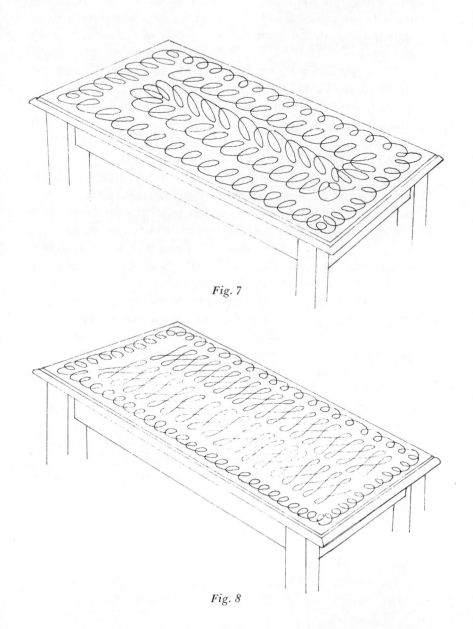

Fig. 7

Fig. 8

the work; and finally use straight strokes. The oil keeps the movements smooth, and the movements themselves are designed to create an even surface, with no polish piling up into ridges.

Now you need a "rubber," which is a pad of wadding shaped like the fad and covered by washed linen (see Fig. 9) ; the polish from now on goes on the wadding, so that it is filtered through the linen. When the rubber is made, test it first on another piece of wood to get it running smoothly.

It is fatal if any oil is left under a layer of French polish as the oil breaks through the surface eventually, causing cracking and ruining the whole job. So the rubber is first used to mop up the surplus oil left from the fadding; fill it with polish and use it in circular movements, ending up with straight strokes along the grain. Oil can be seen as a slightly misty layer. Continue rubbing until any misty film has quite gone and a bright shellac surface remains.

The next stage is bodying, which means building up a solid body of polish. Dab linseed oil on the wood, fill the rubber up with polish so that a bit oozes out when it is pressed, and use the figure eight and circular movements as before. Experts say you should now feel "as much resistance as when rubbing a dry hand over a dry mirror." About three layers are normal, each one requiring the classic movements and ending with an oil-free polish along the length of the grain. At the very end, finish by rubbing a fine sandpaper very lightly over the surface with some oil.

The final stage in the process is removing the oil while keeping the polish. There are three methods—stiffing, spiriting, or aciding.

The last can be discounted, as it is very tricky. You may likewise ignore spiriting, which is not particularly easy either. If you want to try spiriting, work with half spirit and half polish on the rubber, starting with circular movements, then figure eights, and finishing with straight strokes along the

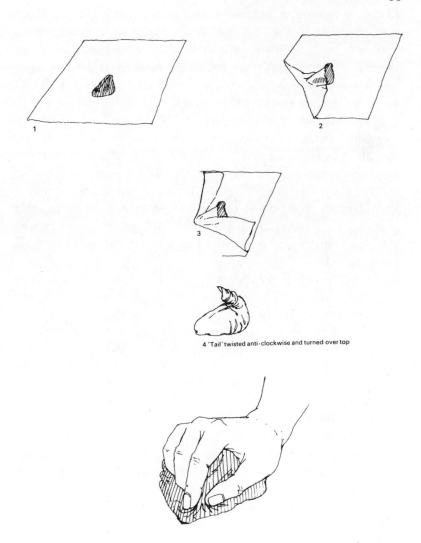

4 'Tail' twisted anti-clockwise and turned over top

Fig. 9

grain. The spirit picks up the oil, but it will also disturb the polish and ruin the job if it is not very carefully handled.

Stiffing uses just a polish-soaked rubber. The name comes

from the feeling of increased stiffness in moving the rubber over the work as the oil is taken up. Make up a new rubber, and apply the polish gently in long sweeping strokes along the grain, decreasing the pressure gradually. It sounds easy, but in fact it's quite difficult to judge the rate at which the oil is being absorbed and the point at which to stop.

Small bits and moldings have to be treated in a different way. The problem is that, however carefully you apply the polish, it is likely to sink into crevices and form a pool. So you have to cheat a bit. Paint on two layers of French polish followed by a layer of varnish. To clear out crevices, mix a small amount of polish, oil, and super-fine pumice powder together on a fad and work it over. The pumice powder will cut down any surplus polish. Finish by wiping off any remaining oil.

When French polishing, it is difficult to know at first how much polish and oil to apply at each stage. Annoying though the answer is, it *is* just a matter of experience. Adjusting the amount of polish is perhaps more important than determining the amount of the oil; if there is too little polish at some stage, the fad or rubber will drag, leaving ugly marks; the polish will build up in ridges if too much is used.

Other Finishes

Although not often used, a linseed oil finish can be useful. Linseed oil, which comes from the seed of the flax plant, absorbs oxygen from the air and dries into an extremely hard layer, heatproof, stainproof, and waterproof. Boiling makes it dry out faster. Obviously this could be very useful on something like a dining table. However, there is a snag; each layer of linseed oil absorbs a certain amount of dust and smoke from the air, so that the wood ends up quite a bit darker than you might have anticipated. However, for anyone who wants to use this finish, here is the formula.

Buy boiled linseed oil. Combine oil with *real* turpentine

in a ratio of 4 to 1 (e.g., cut 4 quarts of oil with 1 of turpentine). Pour into a tightly capped bottle. Apply with a
cloth pad wrapped around a block of wood, which will help
to force the oil into the pores. You will need to do this once
a day for about six weeks; the idea is to put on just enough
oil each time to dry in twenty-four hours, since each layer
must be completely dry before the next goes on.

For those wanting to have fun with a rather new-looking
piece of oak (possibly a 1920s or 1930s vintage), weathering
oak, in order to make it look aged, is comparatively simple.

Dissolve 2 oz. am. potash in 1 pint of water, brush on,
leave for about half an hour, then rinse with cold water and
wipe dry. Then dissolve 4 oz. chloride of lime in a pint of
water and cool, strain, and literally scrub it into the wood.
You will have to wait until the wood is dry to see the true
color (if there is a slight white mist it can be removed with
sandpaper). The lime treatment can be repeated if you want
to darken the wood further, even several times if necessary.
You can't French polish on top, so just apply a wax finish.

This brings up the question of wax as a finish. It is the oldest finish and was used exclusively until the discovery of
French polish in about 1830. Beeswax certainly gives a lovely
warm, mat look, but it's a terrific nuisance to build up a complete finish, and it will always show marks badly. You can
cheat, however, by applying a couple of layers of French
polish to start off with, and building up a beeswax on top of
this.

This is Sheraton's recipe from his *Cabinet Directory of
1803:*

". . . take bees wax and a small quantity of turpentine in
a clean earthen pan, and set it over a fire till the wax unites
with the turpentine, which it will do by constant stirring
about; add to this a little red lead finely ground upon a stone,
together with a small portion of fine Oxford ochre, to bring
the whole to the color of brisk mahogany. Lastly, when you

take it off the fire, add a little copal varnish to it, and mix it well together, then turn the whole into a basin of water, and while it is yet warm, work it into a ball, with which the brush is to be rubbed as before observed. And observe, with a ball of wax and brush kept for this purpose entirely, furniture in general may be kept in good order."

I like "brisk mahogany." Anyway, for a modern recipe, melt a block of beeswax and mix with it twice as much turpentine (real) ; apply it with a stiff shoe brush, letting the turpentine dry out each time before the next application. How long you go on doing it depends on your strength and the depth of shine desired; it could take months to build up a good polish.

Any inlaid wood needs treating with special care, since it is all too easy to damage or dislodge the inlays, and it is an expensive business to have them replaced. Sometimes when they feel slightly loose it simply means that the glue has dried too hard; ironing gently over a thick cloth will remelt the glue. If for any reason an inlay needs to be removed (if it has loosened, and dirt had lodged underneath, perhaps) , soak a cloth in boiling water, wring it out, and lay it over the inlay until the glue has melted. More often than not, a dislodged inlay starts to warp, and correcting this is definitely a job for the expert.

If you are lucky enough to own furniture with perfect inlay, don't rub it with polish of any kind, as this might catch the edges; just wipe the furniture with mineral oil.

Woodworm

"Woodworm" has a death toll sound about it, like "black plague," and I think a lot of people prefer not to think about it. However, there is a certain amount of preventive action that can be taken.

The woodworm beetle itself is an insidious creature, with

a life cycle that would be fascinating if it weren't so destructive. The adult female lays her eggs in wood crevices, and when the eggs hatch, after just over a month, the larvae slowly eat their way through the wood. Slowly is the operative word, since they can do this for anything between three and five *years*. All this time the poor, unsuspecting owner of the furniture cannot see anything unusual, unless he catches sight of minute amounts of sawdust that might be thrown up by this tunneling.

Then in spring or early summer the larvae eat their way to the surface of the wood, change into a chrysalides, and hatch into small beetles. It is only now that the unmistakable woodworm holes appear—as the adult beetles proceed to eat their way out of the furniture and into the open air. Here they fly freely and are back into furniture within a few days, laying their eggs and starting the whole cycle again.

Even the exit holes cannot tell fully the amount of damage the larvae have left behind them—the bugs can literally eat away the inside so that the wood, when it is tapped, sounds hollow.

Although the furniture owner sounds defenseless, there are chances of both defense and cure. In the first instance, the beetle likes certain conditions: a crevice or roughness in the wood to lay the eggs in; softwoods (particularly made into three-ply) ; and dust, damp, or dirt. So it is worth inspecting every inch of furniture, underneath and inside, to see if there is any wood that has these characteristics (look particularly at the wood backing chests of drawers, wardrobes, desks, and anything else that is heavy and tends never to be moved) . Look, too, at the backs of pictures, where cheap wood is often used as a backing. If there is a piece of wood that qualifies as a likely meal for woodworms, sand it down well, treat it with woodworm fluid, and seal it with silicone.

If woodworm is detected, either from the holes in the

furniture or little piles of fresh sawdust on the floor, redouble
this search for the next possible laying place. Treat the holes
thoroughly with a fluid, because there may well still be
larvae inside, ready to come out a bit later or the following
year. Fill the holes with wax and keep watch to see if the
fluid has done its job (the beetles will eat through the wax
if they are still there). When you're sure the furniture is free
of infestation, fill the holes in securely with plastic wood or
brummer stopping so that the flying beetles have no chance
of laying their eggs there again.

Castors

As with so many things, the choice of castors in ordinary
hardware shops is now limited. But if you have a good piece
of furniture, it is worth searching out the right kind, both for
aesthetic and for practical reasons. Castors put strain on the
legs, and the wrong kind can cause damage. In particular, be
very careful about using screws, as it is all too easy to split
the wood (for the four principal kinds of castors, see Fig.
10). A straight leg can take a central screws, as in Figure 11,
but if there is any curve in the leg, the castor must go over

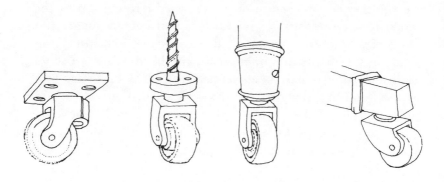

Fig. 10

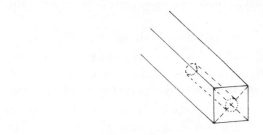

Fig. 11

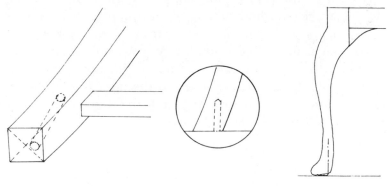

Fig. 12

the central point of the whole leg, not the central point of the
foot (see Fig. 12).

Professional Help

I have referred throughout to "the expert," "the professional," but when it comes to the crunch and a piece of
furniture has to go to one for treatment, it's not a simple
matter of looking up the nearest French polisher and carting
the piece over. Partly from personal experience, and partly

from conversations, I have realized that professionals come in as many varieties as finishes, with varying degrees of skill. The problem is not just to find a restorer, but to find the right person for the job.

I know of one man who will do a basic job cheaply, but he has no understanding or appreciation of antique furniture; another who is a craftsman but somewhat slow and elderly; another who has a staff of about eight, works mainly for the trade, and handles a wide range of furniture from basic Victorian right up to the four-figure antiquarian; another who has a large staff and only handles really valuable pieces, with nothing in the place worth less than $250.

Obviously, the person you employ depends on the value of your article and how much you are prepared to spend. I would suggest asking at the best furniture shop you know for a recommendation (but don't be conned into parting with the piece by stories of "Oh, it's not worth doing anything about . . ."). Other than that, go to the most intelligent restorer; manual work it may appear to be, but brain power will make all the difference between a good and a bad job.

2 Upholstery

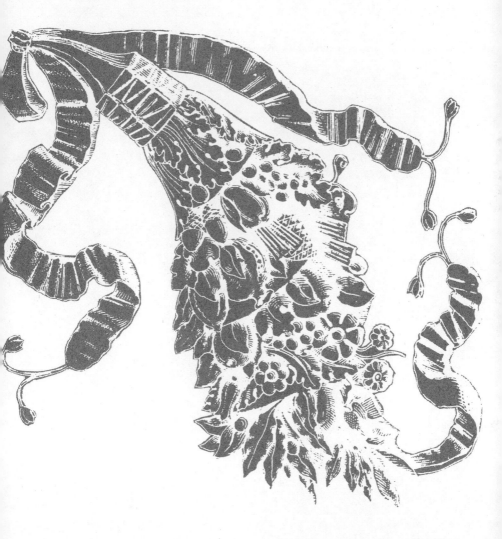

The public on the whole suffers from a great misunderstanding about upholstery. People have visions of turning grandma's old chesterfield into a red velvet button-back, so they go to the local upholsterer. They expect an estimate of about $50 and are absolutely staggered when they are told the charge will be $350, plus the cost of materials.

I know, because I did exactly that myself. Now I am sadder and wiser—wiser in particular about the time and skill that goes into good quality upholstery.

I had imagined it would just mean cutting off the old cover, giving the stuffing a heave to cure the sagging, whisking the scissors over the fabric, running the sewing machine along, and there you are. But really all I am presenting is a frame and a pile of dirty horsehair; as far as the upholsterer is concerned, there's no point in putting a good cover on decayed insides, and if he's going to do the job at all, he wants to do it completely. This means building up a new piece of furniture.

Let me hasten to add that you can always find someone to

do a cheap job, but you get what you pay for; if the chesterfield has already lasted seventy-odd years, it might as well
be given another seventy years of life.

The working parts inside a chair are far more complicated
than the user realizes (see Fig. 13). First my chesterfield
would be stripped right down to the frame, and since there
may be several thousand tacks to be removed, this is no rapid
job.

Then the webbing would be replaced (each web would
have twelve tacks), and the springs stitched onto the webbing, each one by hand (there's little point in replacing just
the few springs that are weak, because the new ones would

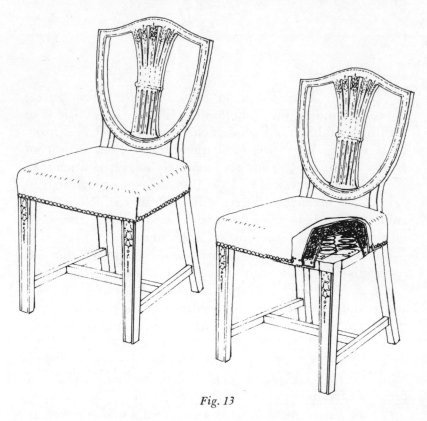

Fig. 13

stand up higher than the old ones) . These are covered with hessian, and loops are sewn around the edges to keep the stuffing in.

The horsehair will have been washed, dried, and teased out again; it is then stuffed tightly under the loops and loosely in the center. A scrim cover is then put over, and the whole seat needs up to six rows of stitching along the front; the stitching distinguishes good upholstery from bad, because the more plentiful and better they are, the longer the piece will keep its shape. Some rows are "blind," that is, the stitches are not fully visible, but the threads are pulling the horsehair into shape inside; some are tight running stitches, making what look like ridges along the front. All are done by hand. Another layer of stuffing is put on and then a layer of calico.

The whole process has to be repeated with the back and each arm. The trickiest job is yet to come—marking out the velvet for buttoning. This requires mathematical precision. First, diamonds are marked out on the back hessian, and then on the velvet, allowing just enough material for the button to pull it taut; if there is a mistake of only one-eighth inch here, the whole series will come out crooked, thus ruining the entire job. The velvet then has to be cut out, stitched, and fitted smoothly on.

All in all, covering my chesterfield would take about sixty hours, which puts the $350 into a different perspective.

I had also had a quote of $140, but, as a specialist pointed out, there is a quick and cheap way and a complete and more expensive way. The quick will last perhaps five years; the slow, for fifty or more. The quick method will bring temporary satisfaction, but the slow will achieve lasting results.

At every stage of the job there is a difference between the two methods: the quick will leave gaps between the webbing, but the slow will fill the whole area in; the quick will shape a button back with plywood and foam rubber, while the slow will actually pull the shape in with the buttons; the quick will use a variety of cheap fillings—fiber, rubbing, hair and fiber mix, rubberized hair—which have a limited life and, in the first two instances, break up badly, but the slow will use just horsehair, which has a marvelous natural curl and bounce and is still springy even 250 years later, but is now expensive; the quick will hold the front up with a block of wood, while the slow will build it up by stitching.

So when having anything reupholstered, check carefully what is being done. For a pretty bedroom chair that will

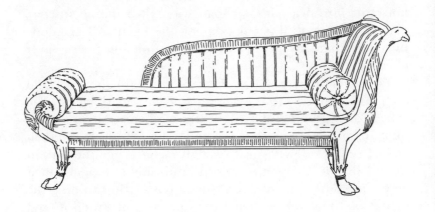

hardly ever be sat in, it would be worth economizing. But for a chair that is going to be used regularly, the quick method would be false economy in the long run.

No amateur is going to tackle a chesterfield—in fact, he would be mad to try anything·with stuffed arms or backs because cutting out the patterns is extremely difficult. However, a dining chair or occasional chair with stuffing only in the seat is quite within the realm of possibility, if the amateur has the space and patience.

The first great problem is buying the equipment and materials, because the right ones must be used, and, on the whole, they are unlikely to be stocked by the general hardware store. Likewise, upholstery suppliers are not very happy about serving the general public.

You need:
> A cabriole hammer, which has a small head and a split at the other end to remove tacks.
>
> A web stretcher or strainer, which is basically a piece of wood over which webbing is pulled firm.
>
> A spring needle, which is large and curved and used for sewing on the springs.
>
> A double-ended bayonet needle, which stitches through large areas of stuffing.
>
> A regulator, which is like a long bodkin and distributes the stuffing after the under-cover has been put on.
>
> Skewers, useful to hold material in place before tacking.
>
> Mallet and chisel for removing obstinate tacks.

The materials used are:
> Webbing: The best is called Jude webbing. A new kind called Pirelli, which has rubber enmeshed in two layers of fabric, looks like the answer to an amateur's prayer since it stretches, but in fact it should be used only on seats that have rubber cushions.
>
> Springs: In the good old days, these used to be made entirely of copper; then copper-plated steel was used, but now they are usually just lacquered steel. They come in various gauges, from 2 in. to 14 in.
>
> Tarpaulin canvas: A heavy type of hessian that usually comes in 72-in. widths, used to cover the springs.
>
> Scrim: A loose type of canvas that goes over the first horsehair stuffing.
>
> Calico: A cotton that goes over the second stuffing.

Twine: Use the best for a long-lasting job—spring twine for sewing on the springs and sewing twine for stitching the edges.

Tacks: ⅝ in. for webbing and ½ in. for the cover—make sure they are the "improved" variety with larger heads.

Gimp pins: For attaching the braid.

Remove the old cover and webbing, taking care not to split the frame when removing the tacks. The old horsehair will look revoltingly dirty; carry it gently to the sink and run cold water through until no more dirt appears, dry it spread out on newspaper in an airing cupboard, and pull it apart until it is loose and springy again.

Check the frame for any weaknesses; it takes an enormous number of tacks, so strain is not surprising (see furniture chapter for frame repairs).

If the chair has springs, the webbing goes underneath the springs; if it has no springs and is being "top stuffed," it should be attached to the top.

Mark where the webbing is to go and start tacking at the back of the chair, first tacking the end down so that it goes away from you, then turning it over and tacking it again so that it is now folded toward the front.

Now the web strainer comes into action. The idea is not to stretch the web as tight as it will go, which will only end up splitting it, but to stretch it tighter than mere hand pressure could. There are two varieties of strainer—one with a slot through the top and one with teeth or a rough edge at the end that grips the webbing. Whichever variety is used, hold it in an upright position, hold the webbing taut over it, and pull the strainer down to an angle of about 45 degrees. (See Fig. 14.)

Now you have to do a bit of juggling to get the tacks in,

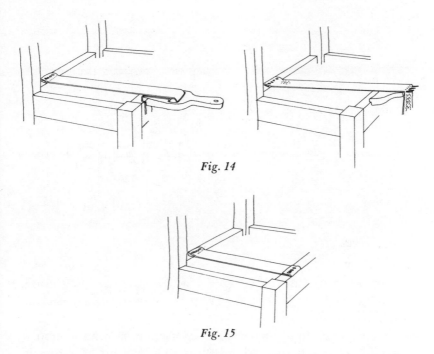

Fig. 14

Fig. 15

pushing one in with the right hand thumb, and switching hands and releasing the strainer while you switch hands to hammer the tack in. In fact, it is a good thing if a bit of pressure comes off the webbing at this point because if it is literally stretched to its limit, it will split when the chair is used. The right amount of stretching will, I am afraid, only come with practice—although you might be lucky the first time. Turn the end of the web over and tack it down (see Fig. 15).

When the whole chair has been webbed (and the webs should be closer together toward the front of the seat), mark out where the springs are to go. Allow about 1½ in. between each one and stand them on webbing, rather than gaps, as far as possible. Each spring has a very marked joint at the bottom where the steel is tied off (see Fig. 16) —have these

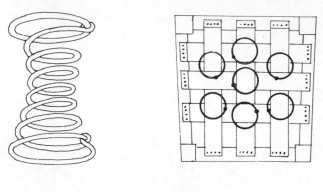

Fig. 16   Fig. 17

facing towards the center (see Fig. 17) so that they don't work through the hessian covering by uneven pressure when the chair is used.

Each spring should have three knots, and each knot should be tied separately (see Fig. 18) so that if a bit of twine is rubbed through, the whole lot will not come loose.

This particular chair uses seven 6-in. springs, which are spread more toward the front of the seat than the back, because that is where the most pressure will be.

Fig. 18

When all the springs are in place, they need lashing together in the correct position. Secure the end of twine with
a tack at the edge of the chair; then tie the twine around a
row of springs, taking it around each one in turn; use the
knot (see Fig. 19) and take care to keep the springs in the
position that is illustrated (see Fig. 20). This is very important, because springs at the wrong angle will give the
chair the wrong shape.

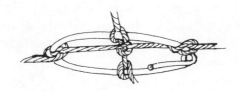

Fig. 19

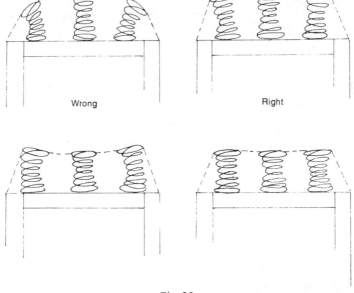

Fig. 20

Cover the springs with tarpaulin canvas cut to the seat shape with an inch overlap; this is turned in and upwards before it is tacked down. Stitch the springs to the canvas in the same way that they were stitched to the webbing.

Now the stuffing loops are sewn around the edges (see Fig. 21). These go about 1½ in. from the edge, each loop just loose enough to allow a hand through. Each stitch should be secured separately. Stuffing the horsehair under is more difficult than it might appear; the aim is to get it tight and even, and it's best to do a small amount at a time. The twine will eventually be embedded in the hair. When the edge has been done, fill the center in with horsehair quite loosely (there are no stitches to keep this in).

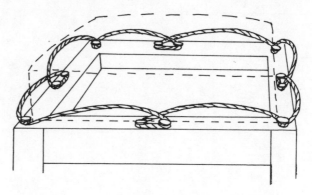

Fig. 21

Cover with scrim in the same way as the tarpaulin canvas, keeping the threads straight and pushing the hair into it, rather than pulling the canvas down over the hair. Cut into the corners by folding the corner over onto the seat of the chair (see Fig. 22). If any part of the stuffing looks bumpy, use the regulator to maneuver the horsehair—pushing it as far to the front as possible.

To keep the stuffing into the edges, make large running stitches right through the seat about a third of the way in

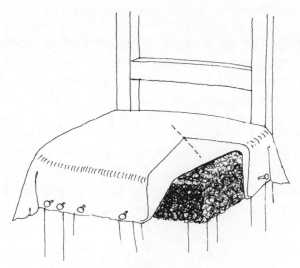

Fig. 22

Fig. 23

(see Fig. 23). Try to avoid passing the twine close to the springs.

Now comes the process known as stitching through, which is both difficult to describe and difficult to illustrate, but not so alarming to do (at least, the basic principle is not difficult, although correct execution is skilled and takes long practice). From the bottom edge of the front, push a needle up to the seat top at an angle of 45 degrees; don't pull it right out, but as soon as the eye appears, push it back down again at an angle of 45 degrees going in the other direction (so that the two needle movements make a triangle (see Fig. 24).

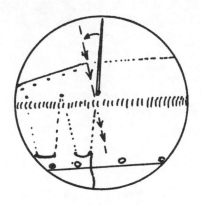

Fig. 24

Pull the needle right out at the base again, and secure the stitch by winding the thread four or five times around the needle before it is pulled tight. Push the needle into the chair again about 2 in. along and repeat the two stitches, each at a 45-degree angle. There will be a row of running stitches visible at the side of the chair and virtually nothing on the top (see Fig. 25a).

Stitching through is very important because it gives the

chair shape and strength. Just how tight the stitching should be pulled is impossible to describe in words or pictures; it is just something that comes with experience. The number of rows is between two and eight, depending on the size of the work; each one should bring the seat a bit farther forward, and there should be enough material and stuffing so that the last row comes out neatly at the right angle. This particular chair will need three rows, the last one being the tight "roll" that any stitching through ends with (se Fig. 25b).

The chair now needs a second stuffing, not as elaborate as the first, but more to bring the shape up to an overall curve. Stitch several rows of stuffing loops from side to side, and wind the hair under them. Then cover the stuffing with a layer of unbleached wadding cut to the chair shape—this will not need securing anywhere. Finally, cover with a layer of calico. This is a much lighter material than the others previously used, and as it is the last layer before the top cover, it must be quite smooth. Don't pull it too tight, or it will end up in folds where the tacks are; just smooth it continuously with your hand from the center outward to keep the tension right.

Put in temporary tacks, starting from the center of the back and leaving the corners free; fold these over and tack them to one side (see Fig. 26). When the whole seat looks and feels quite smooth, knock the tacks right in. Then test your handiwork by sitting on the chair; you should not be aware of any lumps or of the springs grating together.

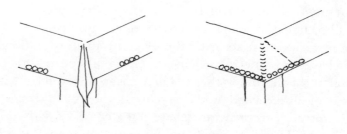

Fig. 26

Cut the top covering about 1½ in. larger than the chair seat (to do a proper job make a pattern first out of calico). Measure the center of the chair and the center of the cover and push a skewer through. Then measure the center of each side, match up to the center sides of the material, and put in temporary tacks. Smooth the fabric down the whole time and use the skewers freely. When you're quite satisfied with the fit, pound the tacks all the way in.

It's worth spending time to make sure it's absolutely smooth, because any unevenness is going to be accentuated by use, and then the cover will have to be refitted.

If you are doing more than one chair, remember that every piece of fabric has a pile which needs to go the same way on all the chairs, particularly if the material is velvet. If velvet goes different ways on two chairs, one will look much darker than the other. Even woven material has a warp and a weft that can make the pattern look different from different sides.

If the material has a pattern that needs centering onto the seat, first cut the shape out of newspaper; then cut out most of the inside so that you're left with a rim that you can move over the pattern until the best section shows through.

Much light Edwardian furniture has what is known as "pin cushion" upholstery—that is just a very light stuffing on webs attached above the seat frame. Web in the way described, tack hessian over, and stitch rows of stuffing loops from side to side. Push the horsehair under, and don't be tempted to build up any more than a slight thickness—this furniture is designed to have very flat seats. Cover with calico (and be careful to keep an eye on possible splits in the frame when tacking, as it is likely to have been made of thin, soft wood).

It's a great temptation in any upholstery to use foam rubber, but it never looks very good and wears down very quickly. So try to use good stuffing.

If the webbing has split, but the rest of the chair is in reasonable condition, it is feasible to redo just the webbing (although the professional upholsterer will regard this as heresy). Turn the chair upside down and rest the legs on something to keep the bottom horizontal and steady. When the old webs have been removed, tack the new ones on as described on page 48. The springs can be left pushing through the gaps in the new webbing until it has been finished; then they are pushed back inside and tied as described on page 50.

This can only be a temporary measure. If the stitching or springs are worn, the seat won't take weight in the right way, and awkward pressure will hasten a break in the webbing again. But it could be adequate first-aid treatment for a chair that is not used very often.

3 Painting and Framing

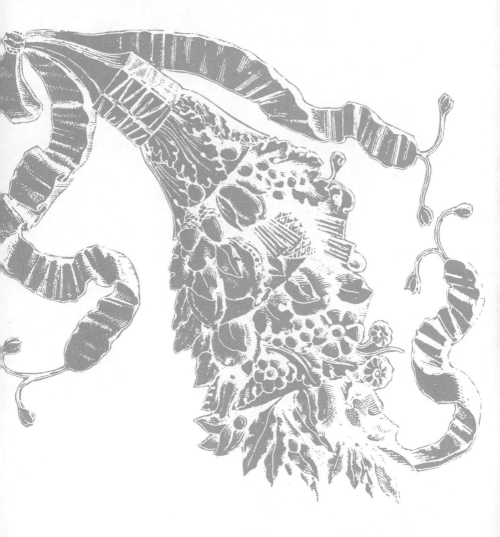

Frames, taken largely for granted, are the forgotten part of art. But of course they can make or mar a picture. At its highest level, framing is an art equal to painting the picture itself.

If a picture of any age needs a frame, it would be nice to find one of a similar age and style, but this unfortunately is hardly ever possible. There are certainly plenty around in secondhand shops and auctions, often framing monstrous Victorian prints or very poor copies of famous paintings, but it is very rare for one of the right size and style to turn up. Although art dealers keep a supply of spare frames, these are more precious than any money and cannot be bought easily, if at all.

The best old gilded frames will have a carved wood base with gesso on top; these can be valuable as antiques in their own right. More often, however, the decoration will be made out of a "composition," gesso mixed with a hardener.

However the gilded frame has been made, it will be very difficult to cut it down, as both gesso and composition will come off in large chunks. Even quite simple frames with no problems or ornate corners will tend to flake. Moreover, the correct 45-degree angle for the corners can be cut only with the help of a miter box, which is an expensive piece of equipment to buy unless it is going to be used regularly. So you may be better off to buy or make a new frame.

Framers will either do the whole job for you, or supply the molding for you to make up. In general, unless you are going to make many frames, it is hardly worth investing in the equipment to do your own, but you might be able to borrow it. Moreover, a professional framer will make "tongues" for the corners (see Fig. 27), a process which is stronger than the usual amateur method of gluing and nailing. But despite the snags, there is the satisfaction of seeing your own handiwork on the wall.

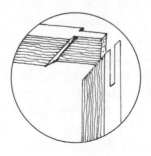

Fig. 27

As I said, the most important piece of equipment is the miter box (and having once tried to cut double-glazed moldings without one, I can assure you it is essential). The cheapest miter box is a simple wooden one with grooves cut in it at right angles; the difficulty is that the saw tends to widen the grooves so that the angle is no longer precise. A metal miter box is more efficient, and a precision version is the best of all, but obviously the price goes up in each case. Apart from that, the rest of the equipment is comparatively simple: a clamp to hold one piece of molding while another is being nailed onto it; a nailset for pushing nails down below the surface of the wood; a very accurate ruler; a hammer; oval nails of the right weight; and wood glue.

Moldings are named according to the shapes made by a cross section. Measure any canvas or panel painting very carefully because it may not be even; test the corners with a T-square, and if they are not exactly square, accommodate the warp in the frame rather than force it back to even shape. A frame should never fit too tightly; it must allow for the painting to contract and expand with the atmosphere. A frame is measured either inside the rebate (see Fig. 28) or inside the front frame (the first is called a rebate measurement; the second, a sight measurement). Make sure you and the framer are talking about the same thing if he doesn't have the painting to use as a guide.

Choosing the right molding is very important. The frame should complement the picture, not dominate it, and, although personal taste comes into the choice, there are certain basic laws. A small painting needs good width around it; the

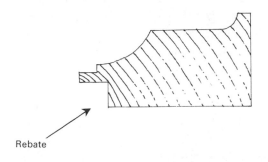

Rebate

Fig. 28

frame for a portrait should pick up the flesh tints, while for an interior it should angle towards the focal point; an inwardly curved frame will make the painting secret and confidential (this style is particularly good on portraits), while a flat painting without perspective needs a flat frame.

An equally important part of the final composition is the matt, an interior "frame" between frame and picture, which is often necessary in the case of prints, water colors, or delicate paintings to give a softening space around them. This can be a plain white beveled cardboard mount or a board covered in a textured material such as linen or silk.

When you have mitered the moldings, clamp one of the long ends, and knock either two or three nails into a short end so that they are in firmly but not protruding through to the other side (one nail is never any good because the frame will swivel and not be secure). Apply wood glue to both parts of the joint, and hold the two parts together while the nails are knocked in—a tricky operation. Hold the short piece slightly lower, and the nails should bring it up just that much to make the joint flush. Push the nails down below the surface of the wood with a nailset, and fill in the hole with plastic wood.

If the picture is modern and the molding made of good wood, just smooth it down and give it a wax polish. Staining hardly ever looks right since the wood is usually not of good enough quality. If the molding is to be painted, cover it first with a ready mix gesso, or the paint will just be soaked up by the wood. Gesso powder and rabbit skin size are needed—both can be bought from artists' supply shops. Soak the size for about eight hours; then heat it without boiling and add gesso powder until the solution has the consistency of milk. Two coats are needed, the second when the first has dried; the gesso mixture in the meantime must be kept in a special double pan that keeps water warm, as it is unusable when it is cold.

Gold and silver paint look horrible on frames; the colors are far too harsh and metallic. However, the comparatively new products Treasure Silver and Treasure Gold can look reasonable (the latter comes in various shades).

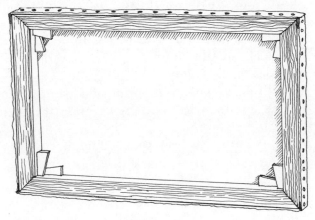

Basic Frame

Beveling a matt board is more difficult than it looks. Use a proper mountcutter's knife—although quite expensive, it will come in handy for other jobs around the house. Put another board underneath the matt when cutting and use a beveled ruler to cut the correct 45-degree angle. Smooth any roughness afterward with fine sandpaper.

If covering the matt with material, stick a rectangle of material right over the front; then cut mitered corners and glue these on to the back. Fine materials such as silk won't stick and will probably have to be sewn around the matt.

Gluing a print or picture onto a mount will automatically decrease its value, so take care when you do it. If you are sure that gluing doesn't matter, use a flour paste and, if possible, smooth the mount on with a roller (a rolling pin will do). Make sure there is just the right amount of paste, because any that oozes out will look ugly. If not using adhesive, secure the picture onto the mount with a small piece of brown strip gummed paper doubled over to form a hinge.

Glass needs to be the special 18 oz. picture glass. Most glass shops should stock it, but you may have to search for it. Wipe it over with alcohol before putting it in. Secure the picture in the frame with small nails, making quite sure that these are not splitting either frame or glass. Cover the back with brown paper, sealing it over with gummed sticky paper. Screw type hooks should be fixed in about a third of the way down the sides of the frame.

An expert approaches every print and painting individually, and it's amazing what a difference original thought can make; with the right frame and slip the picture seems to come to life. Framing has been summed up neatly: "It should not be just an extension of the picture, but an environment for it to live in."

4 Paintings

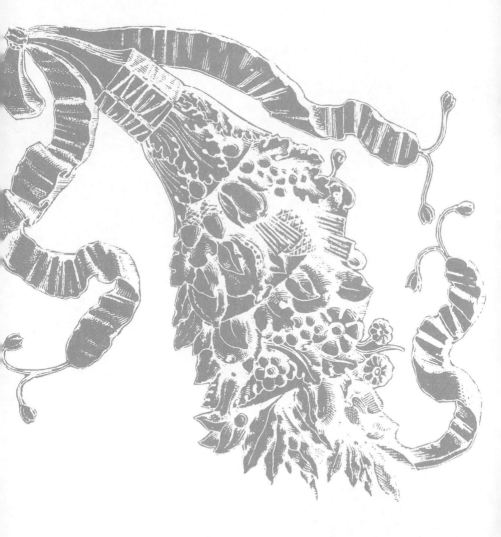

From the scientific point of view, paintings are really very badly designed. Paint is basically a powdered pigment, which in the first instance needs a liquid to hold the grains together; the liquid must dry hard so that the grains can stay together for permanent viewing. The paint needs to be a solid base to hold it in place, and it needs a covering to protect it from dirt and the elements. All of these layers make quite a simple sandwich (see Fig. 29).

The trouble is that to carry out this plan, some very unstable and dissimilar materials are brought together, and the combination invariably results in detrimental changes.

Many pigment materials have been used in the history of paintings—some natural, some synthetic. The natural ones come straight from the earth (ochers and umbers, for instance, owe their colors to iron). Some, such as white lead or cobalt blue, come from metal oxides, while synthetic pigments, such as bitumen brown, are industrial by-products.

When the pigment has been turned into powdered grains, it is mixed in a medium, and here again the materials vary.

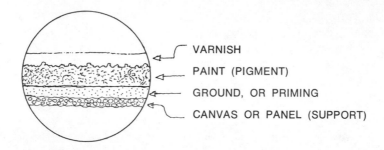

VARNISH

PAINT (PIGMENT)

GROUND, OR PRIMING

CANVAS OR PANEL (SUPPORT)

Fig. 29

For a water paint it will be an aqueous solution of gum, which evaporates and returns to its original hard state. For oil paint, it will be oil from a plant—flax, linseed, or poppy are the most common—and here the hardening actually comes from a chemical change, with the oil oxidizing in the air. Finally, tempera is an odd hybrid, an emulsion (like milk) that is a stable mixture of water and oil; egg yolk is the most popular medium, giving a slightly glossy finish to the pigment.

The mixture of pigment can be compared to concrete, with grains being held in a solid matter; the texture of the paint depends on the balance between grains and dried oil. In other words, when there is a high proportion of pigment, the paint will be mat (or lean) ; when there is a high proportion of medium, it will be glossy (or rich) .

The most common support for the paint is a canvas, which is normally linen. The paint cannot come into direct contact with it, because the fabric would absorb oil out of the paint and leave it powdery. Therefore, two more layers are applied to give separation: the first is a glue size (usually made of animal glue) ; and the second is a priming of gesso, white lead, or more commonly a mixture of the two.

To keep the canvas taut it is usually "stretched," that is, tacked over a frame and two wedges knocked into each corner at the back.

A wide variety of materials have been used to make the protective layer over the paint. The word "varnish" is used as a general term to describe them all and is not strictly accurate. Usually a form of resin is used, either hard (made from amber or other hard resins) or soft (made from dammar or mastic). These are mixed with a solvent (usually turpentine), and they harden when the solvent evaporates. Sometimes a hard resin and oil are heated together and, for about twenty years now, an artificial resin made from plastic has been used with excellent results. Wax also makes a simple covering.

To add to the multitude of layers that are used to make up a painting, an artist will often build up colors on the canvas, using green under flesh colors, for instance, or white or gray for highlights. Some even mix oil and water colors on the same canvas!

So many things can go wrong with a painting that it seems as though a fat medical dictionary is necessary to detail them all. It is only comparatively recently that scientific research has been carried out into what, after all, is a chemically complicated subject. Even now not everything is known about a painting's behavior over a period of time.

In the first instance, a painting can suffer simply because it is composed of several layers. Ideally, each layer should be more flexible than the one below—in other words, the one with the most resistance should be at the bottom and the one with the least, at the top. Otherwise, it would be like painting on elastic, then pulling the elastic. But this doesn't always happen, and stress can break up one of the layers if they are uneven.

The density of the layers ought to be evenly graded too— one with coarser grains should be under another with finer grains. But this isn't always so either (I'm sure artists in the full flood of inspiration don't stop to think about the density of their paint) .

Cracking can just be in the varnish, or it can be in the paint layer underneath. If it is in the paint layer, there may be a variety of causes: more oil in one paint layer than the one on top; a second layer of paint being applied before the first has dried; or layers drying at a different rate.

If there is too much oil in the paint, the surface will wrinkle. If there is a faulty balance between pigment and medium, the paint will crumble or break up. Blisters can be caused by layers not agreeing with each other, the canvas rejecting the paint for some reason, or moisture coming through the back.

Pigment can undergo alarming changes, sometimes altering color completely. The rich reds made from madder root or cochineal can fade in the light. The real ultramarine, made from lapis lazuli, fades badly, while the artificial ultramarine, used since the beginning of the nineteenth century, can be decomposed by even minute amounts of acid. Copper green and several dark browns grow gradually darker with time. Alkalis will affect copper resinate greens and can also destroy Prussian blue (which is often used with yellow to make green) .

Lead, either in the priming or in the paint, can cause trouble. Our industrial air inevitably has a certain amount of hydrogen sulfide in it, and this changes white lead into lead sulfide, particularly if the air is damp, darkening the color. Red lead is also darkened by hydrogen sulfide.

Glue and gesso cause an enormous amount of trouble. Glue isn't the stable material it might appear to be—it can shrink and swell according to the humidity, and this movement will loosen the rest of the painting. Gesso is hygroscopic —capable of absorbing water—and will pick up moisture from the wall behind or even from the atmosphere. Once moisture has penetrated, the gesso starts to break up, with a disastrous effect on the painting above it.

The top layer of varnish has probably caused as much damage to paintings as the protection it is supposed to give—not directly, but indirectly, because resin and oil varnish darken with age, and all sorts of vandal methods have been used over the years to correct this darkening. The trouble is that surface dirt is confused with the chemically darkened varnish; although the dirt can be removed without too much difficulty, removing the varnish layers calls for considerable scientific expertise and is not something done quickly and simply at home. In principle, the varnish should be softer and more easily removable than the oil which binds the original paint; but artists in the past have not appreciated the necessity of removing the varnish at some later date. This sometimes makes the restorer's task very difficult. Hard resins are difficult to remove without damaging the paint layer underneath, while the boiled oil and hard resin mix is diabolical. Ordinary removal methods will strip off the original paint, if not the whole picture. Wax is the easiest cover to remove, although it obviously has limitations as a varnish.

Finally, the canvas has its troubles. The material stretches in damp weather and tightens in dry weather, but in the case of a paint canvas, this movement is usually counteracted by the glue in glue size, which makes the canvas behave in the opposite way. All this movement and stress is bad for the painting. Also, canvas attracts mold and of course tears easily.

There is one other problem, the origin of which is still something of a mystery. This is the whitish coating known as "bloom" that sometimes appears on the surface of the painting, occasionally being so bad that the painting is just a fog. Although the actual chemical change has not been fully investigated, it seems to happen only when a painting with a natural soft resin varnish (for example, mastic) has been in an extremely humid atmosphere.

It is obvious that atmospheric conditions affect paintings. In fact, the right atmospheric condition is vital to their life but is often denied them. Humidity is the key here. If the moisture content in the room is too high, mold will form. If it is too low, the dry atmosphere will draw oil out of a painting at a rapid rate (as owners of central heating have discovered to their dismay).

Restoration

It is unlikely that any painting has gone more than fifty years without some restoration. It is quite common to find that someone has retouched the paint over the old varnish, and applied new varnish over the whole surface; when this is removed, the retouching comes off as well, and hitherto hidden damage underneath is revealed. Until our present, more careful age, most restorers in the past tended to prefer the quick effect, not the long-term cure, so all sorts of botching might be there under the dark varnish. Moreover, the more subtle causes of damage were probably not understood; as a result, a painting that has perhaps cracked through from being hung in a drafty place may have been restored and re-hung in the same place, to suffer repeated damage.

There is one horrible aspect of restoring in the last century from which we are still reaping the legacy. This is the matter of the "old master" varnish. Renaissance paintings had darkened so much by the nineteenth century that this brown overall hue was thought to be an original component of classical art. It became desirable on all paintings to such an extent that artists or restorers used a specially brown-tinted "old master" varnish and plunged thousands of paintings into somber obscurity. No one realized that originally classical art had been painted in brilliant, glowing colors until, in comparatively modern times, scientific cleaning methods were applied and hundreds of years of dark veiling were removed.

No mention has yet been made of paintings on wood panels. Here the chances of damage are considerable. Wood is so susceptible to atmospheric conditions, since it shrinks and swells at an alarming rate, that any panel painting is in considerable danger. The older the painting is, the worse the risk, because the painting will have lost its flexibility and will be less capable of withstanding the movement of wood underneath. A picture restorer once showed me an example of damage that ought to be a lesson to all central heating owners. A new system had just been put into a house in which was hanging a small rural scene on a panel; within three weeks a split several inches wide had opened up right across the painting.

As well as unsuitable materials and atmospheric condi-

Carved and Modeled Frame

tions, paintings also have to withstand unsuitable hanging locations. Over the fireplace is probably the preferred location in many houses, but there could not be a worse place. Smoke and fumes rise to leave sooty deposits, and the change of temperature is wide and rapid, with rising heat drawing up cold currents of air.

Additional hazards threaten a painting that is hanging in what appears to be a nice safe spot. Sunlight will harm certain pigments, and if a painting is hanging on a damp or cold wall where condensation occurs, the moisture will penetrate through to the back. Damage can come from improper dusting (if the duster is slightly greasy, it will simply grind the dust in) and weak hanging, which breaks and allows the painting to crash to the floor. Even a speck of dust can act as a focus for condensation of moisture in the atmosphere. So, all things considered, it sometimes seems a miracle we have any art left at all!

When looking at a painting for the first time, make a detailed study of its condition before doing *anything* with it. If the varnish is very dark, dab on a bit of saliva, which will give enough translucence to allow you to see the colors underneath. If there is any sign of the paint's lifting or blistering, handle with the utmost caution. An expert restorer can give immediate first aid to keep the paint from lifting off completely; if the painting looks at all interesting, it is worth leaving it *in situ* and paying for the restorer to come to you. Whatever you do, don't touch the blisters or flakes; if you take the painting to the restorers, keep it face upward, put a board support underneath the canvas, wrap paper around it, and carry it flat.

If a painting ever has to be carried rolled (and it's best to avoid this whenever possible, even if it is in good condition), use as large a roll as possible and keep the paint layer outside, never inside.

If the canvas is slack and the wedges are still there, it

should be possible to tighten it by pushing the wedges in. But this should be done *very* cautiously, because it is all too easy to tear the canvas. A canvas that is too tight or too slack will pick up stretch marks.

If no damage is apparent on the canvas, it is possible to clean off the surface dirt. Home recipes for doing this are legion—wiping with potato, turpentine, linseed oil, and bread are the principal ones. Wiping with a potato is simply applying an alkali, which can be done more effectively with weak ammonia. Although turpentine (either pure or turpentine spirit) will lift off grease, it is also a solvent for many varnishes and could be dangerous if used recklessly, as it may lift off the varnish and start to remove retouching or even original paint underneath.

Linseed oil is *disastrous*—there is no other word for it. It dries into an extremely tough layer, which is completely insoluble and, when it darkens, which it does in a fairly short space of time, it can be removed only by very careful scraping, tiny piece by tiny piece. Moreover, it virtually fuses with the dried oil in the paint, so it requires a very skilled craftsman to avoid damaging the paint while removing the linseed oil. Although linseed oil initially appears to be giving the painting a good cleaning and a polish, you should never use it.

Wiping with bread will do no harm, but it's not a very effective way of removing dirt.

There are various effective patent cleaners on the market. But really just as effective is this cheap home recipe: mix ½ teaspoon of ammonia in a cup of cold water, moisten a piece of cotton wool in the solution, and wipe this over the painting. If the painting has been in a smoky atmosphere, an amazing amount of yellowing and dirt will come off this way to show a much truer and brighter picture.

The painting will then look mat and a bit dull, but it is quite simple to restore a shine. Either wipe on a layer of wax polish and rub it up gently, or, to give a higher gloss, brush over a layer of synthetic resin varnish. As already stated, *don't* use either an oil varnish or linseed oil. Both darken and are virtually impossible to dissolve when they are hard.

If there is mold on the canvas, brush off the surface fluff and keep the painting in a warm dry place for several weeks in order to dry the mold out. There is really nothing to be done about cracks in the paint except elaborate overplanting, which is hardly worth the trouble and the expense. Nor is there anything to be done about a change of color in the pigments. When white lead has darkened, it can be turned back to white by reversing the chemical change with bleach, but this is a skilled, complicated job, which can be done only by an expert. Nothing can be done about darkened red lead.

If the surface of the painting has white bloom, it may disappear with wax polishing; but more often than not, it affects the whole varnish layer, which then must be removed.

Varnish removal counts as a major job and should really be done by an expert. It's all very well to give recipes, but, as was explained earlier, varnishes come in a wide variety, and only professional analysis can tell which solvent is right for a particular painting. The professional restorer will spend a lot of time and equipment analyzing a painting before he even starts to work; he also has the knowledge of painting techniques that will give him a guide to the possible ingredients of the varnish. The problem is that it is all too easy to disturb the paint layer under the varnish (especially if it is softer than the varnish layer), and although the painting might not appear particularly good, it just might be important enough to make this an act of vandalism.

However, if you are quite sure the painting is not of value and you want to try it, you might be able to shift soft varnish with turpentine. Look at the swab after every movement, and if there is a trace of color from the paint, stop the action of the solvent with another swab that has been dipped in ordinary light lubricating oil. Remember that retouching may have varnish underneath it as well as over it, so you may be disappointed to see previous damage emerging as the retouching and old varnish are removed.

Earlier this century a restorer called Pentkoffner produced the magic answer to improving darkened varnish—a box containing a chemical within which the painting was fumed, to reappear with its varnish opaque once again. Unfortunately, this effect didn't last, and the darkness quite rapidly returned. This process is largely discredited now.

The two other major restoration jobs are filling in holes and relining. Although both are preferably professional jobs, the first might be possible at home, again provided you are sure the painting you are tampering with is not of great value. To cover the hole, cut a patch from another piece of canvas (possibly more difficult than it sounds, as artists' suppliers are loath to sell small amounts of canvas). Anyway, obtain a piece, match up the weave as closely as possible, and fix it with heal ball wax.

There are various possible fillers to imitate the original sizing; best is either a woodworker's stopping or a mixture of glue and whiting (with plasticizer). When this has dried, you can have a glorious time exercising your artistic skill at matching in the paint. As in other jobs, fingers are very useful for merging the new in with the old.

Relining is necessary when a canvas has ceased to hold the paint properly or when the canvas itself has weakened; it cannot possibly be done by anyone other than an expert. Beware when having this job done. There are two very distinct methods of relining—one cheap and of limited benefit, the other more expensive but long-lasting. In the first, a new canvas is simply stuck over the back with glue and ironed on; as mentioned previously, glue does no good to a painting, because it swells and shrinks with atmospheric conditions, and the movement puts a strain on the paint layer above. Moreover, the glue does not give real adhesion to flaking paint, which will continue inexorably to become detached from the canvas.

In the second, more thorough method, the new canvas is fixed with a *wax* compound, which penetrates through to the paint layer and gives a real amalgamated adhesion that will last for centuries. Unfortunately, there are more people practicing the first method than the second, so make sure what you're getting when you take a painting in.

Sometimes a painting is in such a bad way, with the paint flaking or curling off fast, that it literally needs first aid. Here the main advice, as in the case of an accident, is don't move the patient, but call in the doctor; in this case, call the restorer, who will immediately cover the front with a protective layer (sometimes paper) to keep the paint intact. The paint can then be secured from the back with the wax compound, and the protective layer can later be removed.

It is sometimes useful to recognize previous relining; compare the weave of canvas showing at the back with that at the front, and, if a second canvas has been added, the difference in size or direction of weave is usually noticeable.

Obviously, prevention is far better than cure, and everyone who owns an original painting, however insignificant they think it is, should take good care. The art market can produce all sorts of seesaw fashions, and that hideous oil moldering in the cellar could suddenly be desirable and worth hundreds.

Hang the painting in a position that is free from drafts, sunlight, and damp. Stick a couple of pieces of cork at the back so that it is not in direct contact with the wall, and the possibility of damage from moisture is lessened. When dusting, slope the top forward and brush gently with a clean cloth.

Always remember that a painting should be treated like a very good piano—take care about the conditions it is kept in and especially about the humidity.

5 Prints

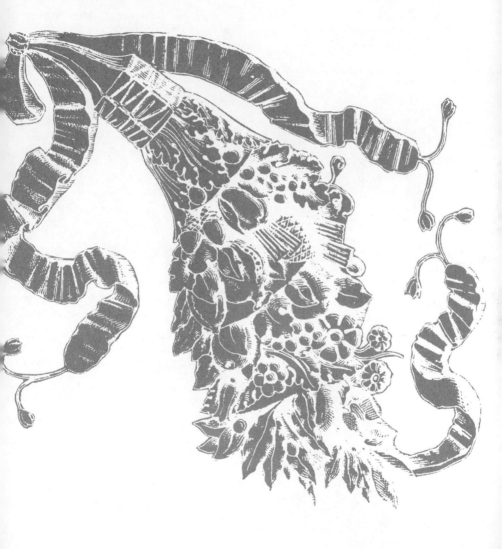

Prints can stand up to a fair amount of treatment, but you must always bear in mind that the materials used for both paper and ink have varied over the years, and even though nine prints take to a process, the tenth just might not.

Before starting to do anything to a print, check up if possible on its value. I must admit I am suggesting something that is difficult; the same design can have been printed for 200 years, and only a very expert eye can tell the exact age of a particular copy. But I should hate anybody to ruin a valuable item for lack of this precaution.

General dirt and pencil marks can be removed either with bread or with an artist's eraser called Artgum. Be generous with the bread, using another bit as soon as the first one is dirty; don't use an ordinary eraser because it will probably be too harsh.

If the print has been stuck on cardboard, and you want to remove it for cleaning, remove the board from the print, not the print from the board. This is somewhat tedious. Cardboard is made up of several layers, and each one down to the last couple should be removed with a knife, sliding along carefully. Then hold the last two in the steam from a kettle, and tear each one gently off with the print lying flat on its face. When the print is clear, there will probably be some glue left, and this must be wiped off, or it will cause the print to pucker later on.

Although it sounds drastic, a soak in cold water will do a lot to brighten a print. Lay the print on a sheet of glass, place it in a flat-bottomed container (a photograper's enamel tray is ideal), and run water in gently. Leave it for an hour, and rinse in hot water. If you can buy distilled water (stocked by grocers) for this and any other treatment, so much the better. Take the *greatest* care with the print all the time it is in the water and especially when lifting it out, because the paper is very fragile when it is wet; slide the glass with the print on it out of the container very slowly at the end. All sorts of stains will probably come off with this simple treatment alone (fly marks and mildew in particular).

A stronger cleaning can be given by soaking the print first in a wetting agent such as Lissapol for half an hour, and then literally washing it. Lay it face down on the glass and use a large soft artist's brush (or better still, a soft shaving brush) to work pure soap gently over the back. Rinse well afterward to remove all the soap from the paper.

Any remaining marks will have to be treated with bleach. Recipes for bleaching prints are frequently given, but print experts regard most of them with horror. For a start, they usually involve dangerous chemicals. Moreover, they can do untold damage to the print, taking all the texture out of the paper and leaving it sparkling white (part of the charm and value of an antique print is its creamy color).

The only safe bleach is Chloramine T, which is strong enough to remove most stains, but mild enough not to harm the print (other bleaches have to be washed out afterwards,

Hogarth Framed Print

but Chloramine T can be left in) . It is sold by most druggists and chemical companies and comes in the form of a white powder. Make a 2% solution with distilled water (¾ oz. of powder in 1 qt. of water) , give the print a few minutes in cold water first, then soak it in the bleach for another few minutes. Finish by drying the print with plenty of white blotting paper.

Whatever you do, don't use household bleach; apart from the damage it might do to the print, it leaves a small and stark look that advertises the treatment immediately.

Wet treatment may remove the size from the paper (or the paper may already be soft and limp, indicating a lack of size) . This can be replaced at home by dipping the paper in a gelatin solution. Dissolve ½ oz. gelatin in a gallon of water, and immerse the print in this for a few minutes, leaving it to dry afterward (remember the previous warning about the fragility of wet paper and treat the print very gently) .

Tears or holes can be mended at home with a bit of patient ingenuity. Paper is made of a mass of woven fibers, so, to a certain extent, these can be "rewoven." In the case of a tear, put the print face down on a piece of glass, immerse it in water, and float the torn pieces together. Slide the print on the glass out of the water and when the tear is still damp, apply pressure to the joint, stroking along the grain of the fibers with the back of a spoon.

The joint can then be secured with paste or a patch. The paste for this and any other sticking of prints should be made with flour, as anything else might damage or stain the paper. Measure 17.5 oz. of flour and 2.6 qts. of water. Mix the flour with a small amount of the water, boil the rest of the water, and add it to the mixture; finish off by gently heating the paste in a double saucepan for ten minutes. The patch should be cut from the same kind of paper (that is, handmade or machine-made). If it is machine-made, the grain must go the same way (to determine this, dampen a corner and watch for the side that buckles—this will be the cross-grain side).

Small holes, especially worm holes, can be filled in—see page 13 for details.

In the nineteenth century it became a practice to give prints an aged look by soaking them in tea or coffee solutions. That may be a good idea for instant antiquing of cheap modern prints, but is not a good practice on anything else unless you are quite sure the print is not of any great value.

Creases can be removed by dampening the paper slightly and ironing it over brown paper with a warm iron (again not something to be undertaken unless you have checked on the value of the print, because you may scorch it). Another method is to wet the print, blot excess water off with blotting paper, put it on a sheet of glass, and attach it to the glass all around the edges with strips of paper covered in flour paste. The print will be kept taut as it dries and tries to shrink.

If you have a valuable print, it can be protected to a certain extent against fungus by wiping over the back with a solution of thymol.

6 Books

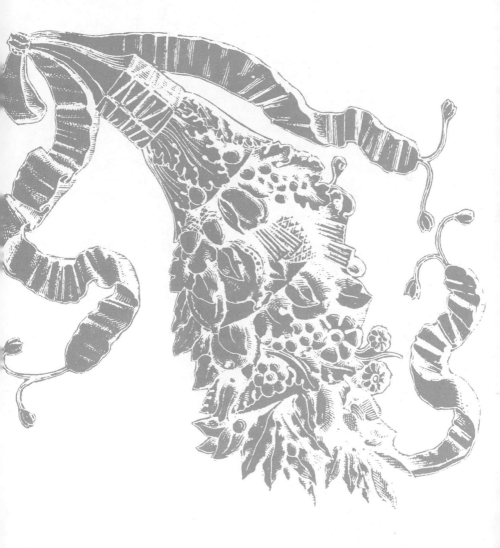

Like furniture, books are also living things (and I don't just mean that the printed word is alive). Both leather and paper are organic substances, affected by heat, humidity, sunshine, and insects. Paper is also hygroscopic, water absorbing. And damage in books is perhaps more insidious than in furniture because books tend to be left on shelves for long periods of time.

The enemies of books are often invisible until it's too late. The atmosphere itself, for instance, can do irreparable harm. If the air is too dry, a leather binding will dry out until it literally crumbles. If the air is too humid, mildew can take hold; this is not just a condition but an actual disease that can rot both binding and paper. Industrialization has brought a new hazard—sulfur dioxide. Leather bindings nearly always have a small amount of iron compounds in them, and these convert sulfur dioxide to sulfur trioxide, which reacts with water to form sulfuric acid. And the ultraviolet rays in sunshine can change the molecular structure of both paper and leather.

It's the third component of books—glue—that attracts insects in the first place, although, once there, they will eat their way through paper and leather quite happily. Oddly enough, the bookworm (yes, there really is one) is not often found in temperate climates; in temperate climates, insects are likely to be small beetles and the aptly named silverfish, which looks attractive but is destructive.

Leather Binding

To add to the book owner's problems, nineteenth century binders often put speed before quality, using leather that had not been properly cured; acid that remained caused the whole binding to disintegrate.

This last problem, making a leather binding that is not self-destructive, was solved sometime in the 1920s, when experiments led to a better method of curing skins; a modern binding, if it is cared for properly, should last a very long time.

You may think that proper care means putting your books in a glass-fronted bookcase. Oddly enough, that is the worst thing you can do. Not only will the books be in stagnant air, but they will miss the one vital aid to proper care of books—handling. As one expert binder said, "Putting a book away is like giving it a death sentence. They need to be fondled."

This is not just sentimental nonsense. The pages need airing every so often to prevent disease or insects taking hold,
and the grease from your hands will help keep a leather binding supple (book men will automatically rub a hand on their
cheeks before picking up a book to make sure of this lubri-
cation).

There are other general rules for book care. Leave a gap
between the books and the wall or the back of the bookcase,
so that air can circulate. Stand them tightly enough to give
each other support, but not so tightly that the bindings are
rubbed. Dust shelves regularly to keep insects away, particularly in warm weather, when they are most likely to appear.

Both temperature and humidity in the room are important—the latter especially so in central heating (high central
heating destroys fine bindings). A hygrometer will help you
to keep an eye on the humidity—it's not foolproof, but it's
better than nothing. Humidifiers over radiators are obviously
a necessity.

Leather bindings need to be kept supple with a dressing,
and here the British Museum Leather Dressing is the classic.
Rub some in about once a year (but be careful not to rub
over gilding, which is pure gold leaf and easily rubbed
away). British Museum Leather Dressing is rather expensive, but it is worth the price. There are other manufactured
leather dressings available (Leather Life, for example), and
most of these products will be effective if used with care. A
simple way of cleaning a dirty binding is to wash over with
a weak solution of flour paste and water, mixed to the consistency of milk; rub neat paste into the edges and corners to
prevent crumbling and finish with a leather dressing.

Pages are most likely to suffer from a defect that is in-
ternal, not external; this is foxing, so called because it manifests itself in foxy red spots. Iron left in the paper after manufacture reacts with a fungus to make marks that are very
difficult to remove. The only hope is to try bleaching (see
print chapter, pages 84–85).

If signs of insects are found in a book, isolate the book from the others immediately. The only cure is to shut it in an air-tight case with a strong disinfectant. Ammonia can be used, but with extreme caution.

Holes in the pages can be invisibly mended by expert restorers, or, if the book is not too valuable, try it yourself. Scrape some paper into a fluff, mix it with flour paste, and fill in the hole. Or boil some paper in gelatin until it is pulpy and mold it in. Simplest of all, chew some paper until it is soggy and press it into the hole.

When that ultimate disaster, a flood, happens, the important thing is to keep the size from the paper from dissolving in the water and gumming up the pages. Press each page assiduously with blotting paper, stand the book upright, and fan the pages out, letting them dry in warm but natural air. The binding will inevitably be ruined, but the pages can be saved.

Figure 30 shows a cross section of a rebinding.

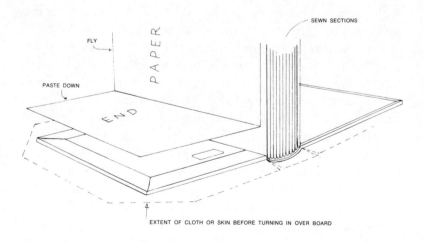

Fig. 30

This brings us to the subject of rebinding (see Fig. 31). As with so many craft trades today, good binders are becoming very scarce, and the demands made on them have greatly increased; you certainly won't be able to take your damaged book in on Monday, order a red morocco cover and pick it up on Friday. There may be a delay now of up to a *year,* and all binders have a vast backlog of work. So a new cover is not a decision to be taken lightly.

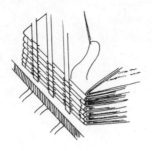

Fig. 31

As in other restoration, there may be more damage than is apparent. The stitching underneath the cover may need renewing as well (see Fig. 31). All the work is done by hand, all of it is skilled, and charges are obviously at a corresponding level (having seen the processes a damaged book goes through, I think rebinding represents good value for money).

The new cover can be in full cloth, full leather, or one of the various combinations known as quarter leather, quarter leather with corners, or half leather. The most commonly used leather is Morocco, which is goatskin. There are two main varities—Niger, which is the finer, and Levant, which comes from a South African goat and is of a coarser texture (used more on the larger books). Calf costs no more, but it has the disadvantage of being easily scratched. However, natural hand-stained calf is by far the best leather for restoring eighteenth century bindings.

Frequently the covers may be in good condition—just unfortunately detached from the rest of the book. This necessitates a very tricky repair. A strip of leather has to be lifted from either side of the spine, and a thin piece of leather glued down underneath. A page that has become loose will, alas, always show, as there are only two ways of repairing it —gluing it to its neighbor or gluing a thin strip of folded paper onto both the loose page and its neighbor (don't forget that there will be another loose page further on in the book, since each one is only half of a folded sheet).

Rebinding can be done by an amateur, and there are books on the subject, but with the value of a wide variety of books soaring all the time, I don't think it's a good idea. The ordinary looking tome you ruin for practice may turn out to be worth a lot of money. For treatment of pages, see the chapter on prints.

7 Metal

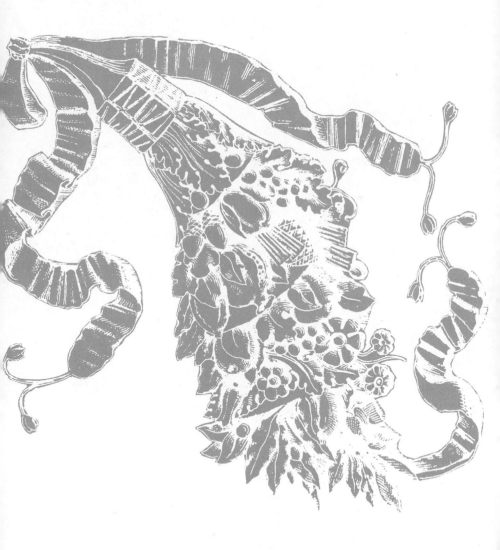

The main metals and their components are:

Brass: an alloy of copper and zinc
Britannia metals: an alloy of tin, antimony, and copper or
  sometimes zinc
Bronze: an alloy of copper and tin
Copper: a pure metal
Iron: a pure metal
Ormolu: a special brass, made for casting from copper and
  zinc or copper, zinc, and tin; usually gilded
Pewter: an alloy of lead and tin
Spelter: a zinc alloy
Steel: an iron alloy

Brass and Copper

Brass and copper are the easiest metals to repair and clean,
but in neither case is it clear sailing.

Cleaning can be done anywhere from the factory to the
kitchen table. The strongest method is sandblasting, which
bombards the article with sand at such a rate that surface dirt

and the pitted layer underneath are literally blasted away. This is used particularly on large objects and is quite an expensive process.

A fair amount of dirt and pitting can be scoured off with a wire wool polishing pad on a buffing wheel. If you can't find a metal worker to do this, sometimes a silver-plater has the right equipment and will oblige. If the object is small enough, a scouring wheel on an ordinary home drill will do the job, but take great care; when you are holding a heavy article such as a copper kettle against the wheel, it's easy to misjudge how much pressure is being applied and to let the wheel catch on a part, with disastrous results both to the object and person.

I use Brillo pads a great deal on metal. They're a bit harsh for some of the decorative objects, but they're quick and can remove a fair amount of tarnish and scale.

A very effective but horrible way of dealing with really dirty items that defy other cleaning methods is to boil them in caustic soda. I've never forgotten trying this in a small flat —the fumes were nearly lethal. However, if you have a gas ring away from the house, caustic soda certainly shifts the dirt. Don't do as I did and put copper and brass in together; the copper, being softer, just plates the brass and is a devil to get off again.

A cautionary note about using caustic—it may get into the pores of the metal and can cause damage. So use it aware of the risks, and rinse the articles well afterward.

Professional firms use acid for cleaning, and, provided great care is taken, this is also possible at home. Use a dip composed of sulfuric and nitric acids, which can be bought ready mixed from cleaning material manufacturers (see page 203) and considerably diluted with water to the required strength. After the article has been dipped, wash it well with clean, cold water, and dry it well before using the polishing wheel on it.

Please beware—you are handling dangerous substances, and great care should be taken. Keep the dip in a non-corrosive container—a polythene dustbin would be suitable. Wear thick rubber gloves, a tough apron (preferably rubber), goggles, and a paint spraying mask with replaceable pads. Never leave the articles in too long, or they will literally be eaten away by the acid.

Finish articles with a polish on the buffing wheel. Some professionals can make machine polishing look like hand polishing, but this refinement is probably beyond the scope of the home operator.

While investigating for this book, I was given a recipe for cleaning metal by one dealer, with a great flourish of pride— he said spread tomato catsup on and leave it. But in fact it is only the vinegar in the catsup that is acting, and then only because it is a mild acid. You could as well mix vinegar with flour or use lemon juice—the effect would be the same. If applying either, wash it off well afterward.

All the brand-name cleaners have an abrasive action, which will also help to rub out scratches in time. If the article is very old and worn, use jeweler's rouge and paraffin, which will be gentler.

It is incredibly difficult to find anyone to mend metal professionally. One specialist explained the problem: with his large overhead, it just wasn't worthwhile doing small, fiddly repair jobs, when his workshop could have a successful business by making the reproduction lamps which are his speciality.

Unfortunately, to do a proper job on metal involves either brazing or welding; both join metal together by melting it, and both need considerable heat (welding, being a complete merging of two parts, needs the most). The heat for brazing could be given by a blow torch, but welding needs an oxy-acetylene torch, which is beyond the means of most small workshops.

Soft solder can be used, but it has disadvantages. The two arts are always likely to spring apart again, and once soft solder has been used on a part, it is impossible to use a hard solder at a later date, because the heat necessary for a hard solder melts the soft and makes it penetrate right into the metal. Removing the soft solder means either cutting out what might be quite a large hunk, or dipping the article in acid, which is complicated and difficult.

Some repairs can be done at home by a mechanically-minded person. Brazing is possible with a simple blow torch, but take care where and how long you apply the heat, as old solder might melt, and the seams might come apart. Soft soldering is also possible with a small soldering iron, but remember the warning above. Hold the article in clamps or blocks during either process, in order to leave your hands free for torch and solder.

After using soft solder, file it down and finish by polishing on the buffing wheel; a polishing mop kept exclusively for either metal will, if used on soft solder, apply a certain amount of real "metal" color to mask the joint.

When hammering, put a sheet of rubber over the metal to prevent any ugly marking (use either a ball knob hammer or a hide-faced hammer). An ordinary household iron makes quite a good anvil.

Cast Brass

Cast brass is a problem metal, because is becomes brittle quickly (despite its substantial look and feel). If hammered, it is quite likely to snap, and brazing or welding is difficult. When straightening a bend, put a hollow rod or pipe over the piece, apply as much heat as possible, and put pressure on the rod or pipe to do the straightening.

Britannia Metal

Britannia metal is rather sad—so many beautifully shaped tea and coffee pots were made in it and silver-plated during the nineteenth century, but it's a terrible metal, and very few of the pieces have survived in good condition. Being very soft, it's easily dented and corroded, and silver-plating has a tendency to scale off it. Moreover, it's a horror to replate, and quite a few platers won't touch it.

When buying any silver-plate, find out if you are buying "hard" metal (for example, nickel) or "soft" (for example, britannia metal, or BM). Hard metal is worth more money, and hard metal prices should not be paid for soft. Britannia metal will often be marked either simply "BM" or "EPBM" (the EP standing for "electro-plate") and has a soft, dull feel when you tap it. When the plating has worn off entirely, BM looks very much like pewter, and, indeed, unscrupulous dealers will pass it off as such. Like pewter, it can be polished up to a dull silver shine and really can look very nice; so if you can't afford pewter, look at the possibilities of Britannia metal.

For repairs, see *Pewter,* pp. 104–105.

Bronze

Bronze is confusing because it doesn't always have that rich brown color. In my early days of trading, I sold what I thought was a brass figure of two boys playing leapfrog, although somehow it looked too good to be brass; the man came back the next week and said how pleased his wife had been with the bronze, and I realized my mistake too late.

I'm still slightly hesitant about telling for sure if a piece is bronze, and I tend to use weight as a guide (on the basis that bronze is heavier than brass), but this test is not infallible. The copper in the alloy gives a reddish tinge, which seems to come out more strongly on some pieces than on others; sometimes it is obvious side by side with a brass piece, but not standing alone. When disposing of possessions, make sure you don't give a bronze to the rummage sale by mistake.

The metal can suffer from what is known as "bronze disease," although this is more likely to happen to really old pieces. It manifests itself in light green spots caused by salts eating their way into the metal. It's not easy to cure. Try soaking the article in water first and if that doesn't work, try a solution of sodium sesquicarbonate.

Never polish bronze with a brand-name metal cleaner, because you will ruin the all-important patina, that rich brown look. If the patina has been removed, it is possible to replace it by using a variety of acids, but this is a professional job.

Brown boot polish is a useful old recipe for keeping bronzes in good condition; being simply a colored wax, it just builds up a protective sheen.

Copper

See *Brass,* pp. 97–100.

Cast Iron

Possibly more damage is done to cast iron than any other metal. Because it looks so strong, it tends to be treated roughly, but in fact, like other cast metals, it is very brittle and will snap easily if dropped or hit.

Unfortunately, it is also a difficult metal to work on. It needs to be preheated, and welding is an extremely difficult job; only a competent man with the right tools is likely to be successful and then probably only on flat articles. The amateur might be able to join broken parts with mild steel plates, but even drilling holes to take the pins is hazardous, so great care must be taken.

If the article is decorative and not valuable enough to warrant a full repair, a certain amount of touching up can be done with iron cement. This is powdered iron filings, bought from ironmongers or builders' merchants, which is mixed with water; it dries hard and can be filed to shape afterward. Holes or cracks can be disguised quite well with it.

Cast iron is usually painted over with black paint, but it can be sand-blasted to a dull metallic color.

Ormolu

Ormolu has usually been gilded; it then becomes tarnished because the brass sweats up through the gilding. Prussic acid is used by professionals to clean the tarnish, but it should not be used by amateurs. Ammonia is the only home remedy—it won't make the ormolu gleam again, but it will vastly improve its appearance. Add a dessertspoonful of ammonia to

Pewter Tankard

a cupful of water, and dab it on sparingly with cotton, rinsing it off afterward with soap and water. Be careful: ammonia has very strong dangerous fumes.

Pewter

Pewter is known as the "poor man's silver," because it can be polished to give a sheen that looks almost like silver. Nowadays the finish for pewter causes a great deal of controversy —to polish or not to polish? Most people on the whole prefer it to look dark and aged and consider the tarnish part of its attractive patina. But there are still some who want pewter, however ancient, to sparkle. It's simply a question of taste, and no one can say which way is right or wrong.

Whoever invented pewter made a very practical metal. It can be filed, scraped, hammered, rubbed, and generally abused, and it will remain whole and attractive. It can even take a soft solder. But *beware*—it has a low melting point, so the surrounding area must be kept cool (a bag of wet sand is useful both to provide the necessary cooling and to act as a prop). And take care how you use the soft solder as it is all too easy to ruin a nice piece that could have been properly repaired by a professional. The best rule is to limit home soldering to small holes.

Never dip pewter in acid, because it leaves a pinkish sheen that is very difficult to remove. Powdering or scaling can only be removed by grinding on the wheel, but a very old recipe for cleaning general dirt off is to boil the pewter with hay; use plenty of water, as it boils away quickly. The result will be an attractive dull sheen.

It is possible to remove scratches or inscriptions simply by scraping with a sharp knife, but the process will leave an ugly dent unless you do it carefully, following the contour of the article and easing the amount removed gradually around the edges. Finish by buffing to disguise the work.

Dents can be removed with reasonable success at home by

using a horn-headed hammer and resting the article on a sand bag. Fortunately, a certain battered look goes well with pewter, so this doesn't need to be as perfect an operation as removing the dents from silver!

Because it is a soft metal, handles, spouts, and rims are often either broken or missing. Don't always discard the article. Sometimes it is possible to scrape off the remaining parts of the break and end up with something that may not be perfect, but is still attractive to look at (a handleless mug, for instance, could be turned into a flower vase).

Spelter

During the Victorian era, thousands, perhaps millions, of items were made in a spelter, a zinc-based metal. Figures, candlesticks, mounts, clocks—you name it, the Victorians made it in spelter. The metal in its natural state looks like tinny lead, but it was adorned with all sorts of coverings— paint, gilding, or bronze among them.

These coverings must cause a lot of disappointment to the uninitiated; how many think they have found a lovely bronze statue, only to be told it's a fraud? In fact, spelter is not a difficult metal to recognize quite rapidly, because it has a very distinctive tinny feel and look. Just tap (but lightly, because it is brittle) and there will be a light "ting"; it is also a very light metal for its bulk, which should identify it right away, unless it has been filled or the base has been weighted.

Unfortunately, although only a commonplace base metal, spelter is more difficult to mend than some more valuable metals. It will never take to solder, as it melts at a low degree; turn the heat just a fraction too high, and your treasure will disappear before your very eyes. The only hope of mending a break is to pin the two parts together and finish off with a paste metal filler (Loy or Plastic Padding).

Spelter can be regilded, but it has to have a gilding solution to itself, because it leaves a deposit which ruins the solution for any other metal, and not all gilders or metal workers can go to these lengths; consequently, it can take time to find someone prepared to do the job. Nor does it always take the regilding; it has a curiously greasy surface, which sometimes throws the new layer off.

Sometimes black boot polish can make a spelter figure look quite attractive and presentable.

Mild Steel

A break in an article can sometimes be mended with soft solder if no stress is going to be applied to it (for example, on something decorative like a candlestick). The metal will usually take well to brazing.

If the article is heavy and is going to be used (for example, a poker), it will have to be welded; if this is not convenient, mend the heavy article with a lapped joint. This is something that the home handyman might well be able to do. File the broken ends so that they can fit together, and drill a pin through. If the spot can be heated bright red afterward and hammered smooth, it will look a very professional job.

Steel takes very well to sandblasting, coming out with a beautiful dull gleam. To clean steel at home, use sandpaper and oil.

General

If a part is missing, it is always possible to have another one cast, but naturally it is a very expensive process. Only a very valuable article will normally justify such an operation.

Never identify a metal by its outward appearance. There are endless permutations of "layers," and a good cut down to the core may be necessary for a final judgment. For example, at the end of the nineteenth century, ornate photo frames were made in cast iron; on top there can be as many as three layers—copper, brass, and gilding. Because the layers are so thick, there is quite a lot of confusion about them (either deliberate or otherwise). I have seen them sold as "solid brass," "solid copper," and even "bronze."

Conversely, bronze may have been either gilded or painted over, so a dig underneath could be to your advantage.

8 Silver Mending and Silver-Plating

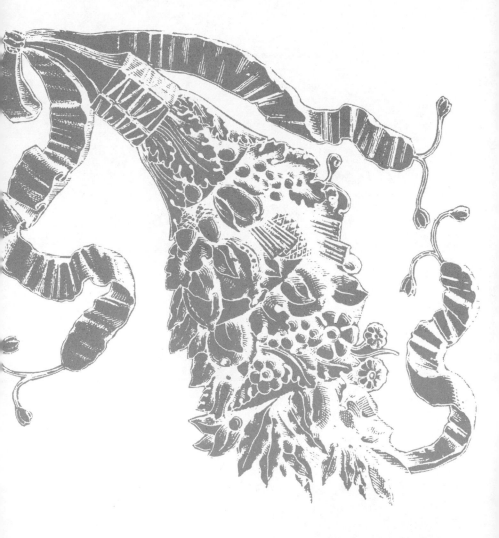

The most important fact to remember about silver is that it is a soft metal. Sterling standard, 925, has 925 parts per 1,000 of pure silver and 75 parts of a harder alloy (manly copper); without the alloy, the silver would be too soft to use. Even with the alloy, silver is not as tough as it appears, and people tend not to treat it with the care it needs. I suppose the thought goes, "Oh well, it's a metal, not glass or china, so it must be strong."

So it gets flicked down by a careless duster, knocked off the table by a baby's groping hand, dropped on the floor, or banged around in the dishwater. The legacy from this treatment is a sad catalogue of dents and splits.

The other damage to silver is chemical. The metal is attacked by hydrogen sulfide in the air to give black silver sulfide (this is activated by moisture in the atmosphere; if silver could be kept in a completely dry atmosphere, it would not tarnish). This tarnish, if left on, will gradually build up until, in extreme cases of corrosion, there can be more sulfide of silver than silver. It is possible to reverse this chemical action, to turn the sulfide back to silver, by treating the article with other chemicals, but this is a laboratory job and usually only carried out on valuable antiquities.

Cleaning

Cleaning normal tarnish from silver is more of a problem than it seems. Brand-name cleaners are basically abrasives, and when they remove the tarnish, they also remove a minute amount of silver; this action, multiplied over the years, can thin an article down quite a bit.

Probably the two oldest methods of cleaning silver are still the best, although I can't see the modern housewife practicing either, given the ease of proprietary cleaners. One method is simply to rub with a thumb; the other is a classic recipe—French chalk made into a paste with alcohol and a few drops of ammonia. Both will still remove a certain amount of silver.

Whichever way you choose, make sure any cloth used is quite free from specks of dirt because particles of dirt will scratch the silver (ideally, the cloth should never be put down on a surface that hasn't been well inspected). And always guard the hallmark well, keeping pressure light and even putting a piece of sticky paper over it (this applies expecially if the piece is antique, as the hallmark can never be replaced: you can't restamp 1746 even if you are quite sure that that was the date). Even an Edwardian hallmark, stamped in an injudicious place, can be worn away with ordinary handling.

Chemical cleaners, in which the silver is dipped into a liquid, dissolve the tarnish without attacking the silver.

It is possible to make your own home dip quite simply. Put soda and a piece of aluminium (a milk bottle top will do) in boiling water, immerse the silver article, and leave until the tarnish has dissolved. Rinse afterward.

Hallmarks

Although it is not possible to restamp an old hallmark, it is possible to have silver reassayed. Silversmiths and retail silver stores can offer advice about this process. The laws about silver are strict. The only kind of silver that can be assayed and described as "sterling" must be 925, or sterling standard. Any lower grades of silver (900, 825, or 800) must be described as such. The finest grade of silver is 999.

Checking on the silver content is difficult, but establishing what sort of silver you have is not difficult. Most jewelers keep a small pot of nitric acid, and with this they can tell you immediately; they scratch a tiny indentation, drop a small amount of acid on it, and the color the metal turns gives the answer—green means it is not silver, a light black means it is a low grade silver, and a dark black means it is a high grade silver.

Silver Teapot

Silver Corrosion

Let us return to the subject of silver corrosion. The chemistry of the damage done to silver by salt is very complex.

Probably the salt first reacts with the *copper* in the alloy; in contact with damp salt, copper probably forms green copper chloride, which in effect removes the copper from the alloy. This leaves the silver in a very porous state, so that, as well as tarnishing, it also develops pits. This uneven surface has to be evened out on a buffing wheel, which removes a certain amount of silver and leaves the article thinner and lighter.

Prevention, not cure, is essential. Blue glass liners prevent direct contact between the silver and the salt, but they are not the complete answer, as salt can be dropped on to the silver in sufficient quantity to cause damage. The only answer is to tip the salt out each day, make sure it is dry, and to wipe the salt cellars with a dry cloth.

Never keep rubber bands around silver because the napthaline in the rubber will tarnish the silver quite severely. Storing silver is an art, with several possible methods. You can buy anti-tarnish paper, or you can make your own anti-tarnish cloth; dissolve 1 oz. of zinc acetate in a pint of water, soak a roll of cotton flannel in it, dry it out completely, and use it to wrap the silver in. Since moisture causes tarnish, a completely dry atmosphere will inhibit it; a moisture-free atmosphere can be created if the silver is placed in self-sealing plastic bags with a little cloth bag of desiccant inside (chemically this is anhydrous sodium or magnesium sulfate; commercially it is silica gel).

Silver Mending

Silver mending is a field in which the decline of restorers seems to have hit the hardest. It's odd because the equipment and skills required are no more complicated for, say, watch repairing; yet finding a good silversmith (or even finding one at all) is an incredibly difficult job. The reason for the scarcity of silversmiths is a complete mystery, and I wish somebody would solve it.

Anyway, if you have found a silversmith, you may be sur-

prised at the comparative complexities of the job. Briefly, it
can be easier to solder on a new part than to remove dents.
I remember I once took in two jobs, a rather dented tea
caddy and a silver pig pin cushion that needed a new foot
and tail. I had expected the first to be quite a cheap job, the
second expensive, but in fact it was the other way around;
the pig cost $2 and the tea caddy, almost $4. When I learned
more about silver repairing, I realized why.

It is relatively quick and easy to solder on a new piece of
silver (the pig's legs weren't very well formed, so it didn't
have to be a work of art). But to remove dents there is no
short cut; the silver has to be "planished," which means
hammered with a special hammer. And it's not just a matter
of knocking the dent straight out; the silver has literally to
be reformed and great care taken that it is not stretched. If
the silver *has* been stretched, it can be hammered thick
again, but this is an extremely skilled operation, which involves holding the hammer at a precise angle and striking the
silver in a precise way. Technically, when a dent is removed,
the silver ought to be returned to the same thickness all
through the piece, and this is not something you achieve
quickly. Some repairers automatically silver-plate a repaired
job to give it a smooth finish.

Although I do a certain amount of dent repairing myself,
I think it's a very touchy job for anyone to attempt on his
own. It's all too easy to misjudge the thickness of silver and
to go right through. However, if the dent looks accessible
and easy, try easing it with something smooth and wooden
(a tool handle or wooden spoon), supporting it from the
back with the other hand. If you lay it down on something
hard, there is a danger of pushing the dent out too far the
other way. At all stages, feel the dent on both sides with your
hand—a better way of judging progress than looking. Sometimes the silver is so thin that you can smooth it with a finger.
If you want to hammer, use one with a horn head.

Candlesticks suffer particularly heavy damage because

they are made by the "spun" method. A wooden mold is formed, a sheet of silver laid over, and the mold is spun around while a steel instrument is held against it. The silver emerges shaped to the mold—and paper thin. Unfortunately, the thinness is masked by the filling of either pitch or plaster and unfortunately, too, if the silver is split or dented, it is extremely difficult to mend.

In the first instance, it takes considerable time to remove the filling without causing further damage to the silver; then the silver is so thin that the solder can't be filed down and polished. Even making an entirely new piece poses problems, because spinners are now few and far between.

So be sure to treat candlesticks with care!

Filling in holes or splits can be a reasonably straightforward job. But beware—make sure hard solder is used. Soft solder is a mixture of tin and lead that has a low enough melting point for a very simple soldering iron to be used. Right after the solder has been applied, it resembles silver to a certain extent, but as soon as it is filed down or polished, the color becomes noticeably darker.

The use of soft solder also has worse drawbacks. For instance, it prevents any later hard soldering being done. The greater heat used for hard solder melts the soft solder, so that it penetrates deep into the silver and it is almost impossible to remove. Removing every scrap of soft solder before doing the hard solder is a very tedious business.

Moreover, the lead in the soft solder forms an alloy with silver that is very easily attacked by the oxygen and sulfides in the air. The alloy becomes very fragile and crumbly, and it looks as if the silver is rotting away.

Perhaps the only time when soft solder can be useful is for filling in tiny holes in very intricately patterned silver (silver hand mirrors and silver-topped dressing table pots, for instance). Here the amount of solder is so small that it is unlikely to damage the surrounding silver, and its use is virtually invisible.

When silver is hard-soldered, the color changes because the great heat oxydizes some of the copper alloy, which comes to the surface in the form of copper oxide. Underneath this is a minutely thin layer of pure silver. Both these have to be polished off, or the color will look peculiar and uneven. Sometimes it is possible to detect that an article has been repaired if you see this coppery sheen along the surface in a good light.

A soft mop on an ordinary home drill (of the Black and Decker variety) can be used to give silver a good polish or to touch up a scuffed surface. With it use jeweler's rouge, a solid block of red compound; or to take out deeper marks, use an abrasive buffing compound. Do take great care, though; the mop removes silver at quite a rate, so look at the work frequently. And make sure there are no odd angles or protrusions coming too near the wheel—if the piece is buffeted by the wheel into the air and on to the floor, all your hard work will be undone.

If you have no wheel, a certain amount of smoothing can be done with wet and dry emery paper (the finest variety) and jeweler's rouge. Finish off with a good rub of a brand-name polish that is abrasive enough to smooth over roughness left by the paper. The finish will not be gleaming, but it may be an improvement—and continuous polishing will gradually bring back a good shine.

I doubt that the amateur can obtain it, but dental amalgam, an alloy of silver and mercury, can make a fair imitation silver for filling in holes.

Silver-Plating

The basic operation of silver-plating is simple enough for a school laboratory to run. Two electrodes are immersed into a solution of silver salts in water. One is the article to be plated, which is connected to the negative terminal of a battery; the other is a bar of pure silver, which is connected to the positive terminal. When an electric current is passed

through, the silver is deposited on the negative electrode
(the article to be plated) from the solution and is replaced
by the pure silver from the positive electrode. However,
producing silver-plating good enough for the home involves
much more in the way of skill and preparation.

It is not a particularly expensive job, so once the base
metal is showing through and beginning to irritate you, there
need be no hesitation about replating. But there are problems, which a description of the process will show.

First, all fitments, such as handles and knobs, have to be
taken off, and this can be tricky because pins have often had
their heads hammered tight. Before the article can go into
the plating tank, it must be quite free from scale or tarnish,
as this would break up through the new plating; muriatic
acid or a newer rust remover is used for the vital cleaning,
and it should be washed off afterward with a detergent.

The condition of the base metal visible at that stage is
vital for the success of replating. Oxidation will show on an
uncleaned article as green spotting, and this may have bitten
into the base metal; sometimes a customer can be very disappointed because the depth of this oxidation is not obvious
from the outside, but if even a small spot has bitten deep into
the metal, replating is impossible without leaving a bad scar.
This is also true of black tarnish, which may likewise have
attacked the metal underneath.

Whether the metal is hard or soft is also very relevant.
Nickel, recognized by the mark EPNS (electroplated nickel
silver) or NS (nickel silver) is hard and poses few problems.
Britannia metal, an amalgam of tin and antimony, is soft and
so difficult to work with that many platers refuse to handle
it. Unfortunately, a lot of the very attractive mid- to late-
Victorian pieces, expecially tea and coffee pots, were made
in it (it is less likely to be marked, but it can be recognized
by a pewter look where the plating is worn) . Apart from scaling and oxidizing badly, it is also much more prone to dents,

which are almost impossible to remove, because the metal has been stretched; as hard as you hammer one out, another appears.

If either nickel or BM has split, the object has to be discarded because the plating invariably widens the split, and soldering is never entirely satisfactory. If you contemplate buying a tea or coffee pot, the key places to look at for weaknesses are at either end of the handle, around the rim of the bottom where the spout joins the body, and on either side of the lid hinge (always hold it up to the light to spot holes normally hidden by shadows).

If the article is sound enough, it is passed to the next stage, a thorough polishing to remove all scratches. This polishing determines also the brightness of the final plating. If any part has been soldered, the object will have to be copperplated first, to prevent the solder from breaking up through the plating. A quick dip into a mercuric salts solution is necessary to prevent a false silver layer from being deposited quickly—it would simply peel off afterward.

The length of time the article should spend in the silver tank determines the thickness of the plating—and also, of course, the cost. You should specify, when you take an article in, what grade of plating you want; something like a coffee pot, which is going to be in regular use, will obviously need a thicker layer than will a purely decorative piece such as a table centerpiece.

Some platers have an automatic brightener in the silver tank; others have to polish off a white bloom to give the final gleam. The articles are than soaked in small pellets of absorbent stone, in order to remove the moisture, and given a final polish.

In the last century, steel was plated by a system known as "close-plating;" the silver was applied with mercury, which was then vaporized to leave the silver layer. This system was used mainly on cutlery, and it meant that knives could have strong steel blades with an attractive silver appearance—an ideal combination. However, the process was poisonous for the workers because of the mercury, and is not practiced nowadays. Moreover, it is extremely difficult to plate non-stainless steel by the present methods, so if you want to re-furbish old cutlery, you may be disappointed.

Americans have a habit of plating all sorts of objects with sentimental attachments—baby shoes, for instance. In fact, as my plating adviser, Mr. Simpkin, said, "you could plate a grape if you wanted to." The object is copperplated first, and the whole process is a nuisance, but the idea might spark off interesting trains of thought.

Opaque Bottle with Silver Stopper and Holder

Sheffield plate causes a great deal of confusion, particu-larly in selling. It was a method used between about 1720 and 1830 to produce cheaper silver articles by cutting down on the silver content; a thin sheet of silver was welded on to one of copper, and the article was then fashioned with the silver side showing. About 1830, silver-plating by electrolysis

was discovered, and, although this may also produce an article with a silver layer on top of copper, there is a vast difference between a Sheffield plated and an electroplated article;
the first is individually made and designed; the second, machine made. To see the difference clearly, take a sample of
each type and compare them; usually the Sheffield plated
article can be distinguished by the seams or the edges where
the silver/copper sheet has been overlapped or turned under.
Needless to say, there is a likewise great difference in value
as Sheffield plate is worth considerably more—really good
examples can approach their silver equivalents in value. To
add to the confusion, English silver-plate is often sold abroad
as "Sheffield plate," because it was often made there, and the
word "Sheffield," has become synonymous with quality. For-
eigners often ask if plate is Sheffield, meaning simply "Is it
good quality English plate?" or "Is it on copper?" As a result,
many dealers label any item plated on copper as "Sheffield"
(and so do many auctioneers).

Anyway, if you have sorted through all these complica-
tions and you have a piece of *true* Sheffield plate, the great
question is whether or not it can be replated. As with polishing pewter, this is just a matter of taste. If a small amount of
copper is showing through and it looks decorative, leave the
article as it is; if most of the silver has worn off and the article
looks messy, have it replated. There will still be the unmistakable signs of Sheffield plate to prevent its being confused
with an ordinary electroplated item.

9 China

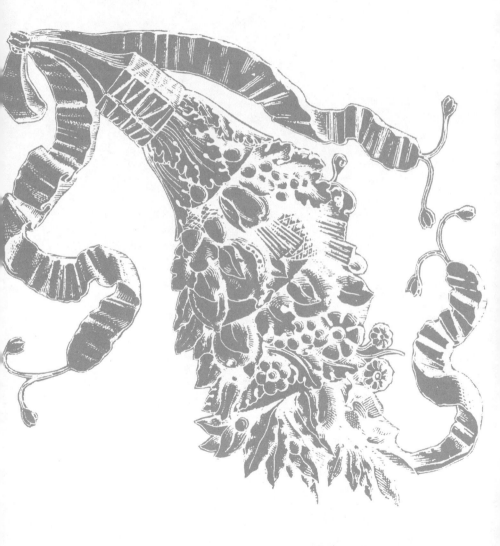

I suppose that part of the reason for the ever increasing value of antique china is its fragility—however careful the owners are, a certain amount must disappear from circulation each year. It is not much consolation, though, to someone who has just broken a piece of eighteenth century Worcester to know that he has marginally increased the value of all the remaining pieces!

There can hardly be a home where someone hasn't at some time looked at a broken piece of china and wondered what to do with it—and hardly anyone who hasn't tried to mend the broken pieces.

In the last few years, there has been almost a boom in china restoring—possibly because the clean, fine work appeals to women. But his has brought about a divergence in standards, and nowadays anybody with a valuable piece that needs restoring should think very hard about where to take it. It is possible to make a repair that looks all right now, but, on a poor job, the new paint will gradually change color so that the repair is very noticeable. To do a repair that lasts requires skill, which some of the newer restorers lack.

The good professional restorer will treat every piece that comes in as an individual item. Restoring processes differ, and most are kept secret; there are no established materials, and each firm has to experiment until it finds its own formula.

The main problem in restoration is that the china can never be refired at the original temperature—the high heat would simply shatter it. So restoration must imitate manufacture, not copy it.

Any missing part can be remodeled, and considerable expertise goes into making sure the design is right—old books, sales catalogues, and museums are consulted if the piece is something new to the firm. Generally, stoving enamels are used for the coloring, and a piece will usually be fired as many as four or five times.

Previous repairs often have to be dismantled first, sometimes creating more work than is at first apparent. Every scrap of old glue has to come out, because even the tiniest particle left in will prevent the making of a clean new joint. A variety of solvents may have to be tried before the right one is found, if the glue is very old, and, at the end, the last bits may have to be picked out by hand.

Taking rivets out is a major repair in itself—what a tragedy it is that rivets were used for a standard method of repair in the nineteenth century (although they do have their uses nowadays on china that is going to be subjected to the stress of constant use) .

Problems can be met at any stage in the process. Sometimes, especially in the case of some porous English porcelain, a stain is under the glaze, and the heat brings it out, causing the stain to darken. Or a stain that is already apparent may become larger. In both cases, eradication is difficult and sometimes impossible. Bisque and parion china are also prone to staining and are equally difficult to repair.

Lustreware colors, because they have been fired originally at very high temperatures, are very difficult to reproduce; for the same reason, so is gilding. In the case of gilding, gold leaf has to be used instead of liquid gold, and the original color can hardly ever be matched exactly.

Underglaze blue is a difficult color to reproduce, especially the subtle shades used by the eighteenth century English factories.

Loving Cup

Regardless of these problems, a nearly invisible repair is usually possible. This brings up the question of "to see or not to see." In other words, should a repair be so good that it deceives? The choice is up to the customer, because the restorer can either mask the damage completely or leave the repair visible to the naked eye. Not surprisingly, dealers tend to prefer the former and collectors the latter!

Although riveting and lacing are discredited now, these processes might still have their advantages when a piece has been broken at a stress point (for example, a handle) but is still going to be used. It is often possible to mask the ties with a filler and paint, so that it need not be an obvious repair.

Certainly, even the strongest glues will not survive unlimited handling in hot water.

How much you do at home depends on the value of the piece, both in the antique market and to you personally. Obviously a good antique should be mended by a professional, but sometimes the broken object is not valuable enough to justify this and just too pretty or treasured to be thrown away. A certain amount of home repair is possible; it will never be invisible, but it can, with care, look quite presentable.

When regluing an old joint that has been constructed clumsily, the most important part of the operation is removing the old glue. Here, time spent removing every scrap will be repaid, because even a tiny alien speck will throw the surfaces out of alignment. Although it sounds drastic, water that has just boiled will shift most glues; keep the pieces that are going to be separated well supported, as they may fall apart with a plop and hit the sides of the container, causing further damage. If the glue still remains, try alcohol and acetone (individually) : the first should dissolve shellac glues; the second, cement glues. Araldite is a great problem, but there is a product on the market called Dissolvex, which should break it down.

Once the pieces are apart, don't assume that all the glue has gone. Because the edges are porous and rough, they will still have glue clinging to them, and this will have to be removed either by further immersion in boiling water or by literally picking the pieces away with a sharp implement (use a needle or a razor). It's all very tedious but necessary. If the edges look at all dirty, soak them in very hot water and detergent with a dash of bleach; it's amazing how even a slight discoloration can mark out the repair line, despite careful sticking.

Before going on to the next stage, let the china dry out completely. Because of its porous nature, this may take as long as a week. Again, there is no point in hurrying over this stage.

Araldite is the best glue now, but it takes some time to harden. The glue goes on far more smoothly if it can be heated slightly beforehand; time spent spreading the smallest possible amount on as smoothly as possible will be repaid by a smooth joint. It's a fallacy that the more glue you use, the better the joint—in fact, the opposite is true.

Cellophane tape is not best for securing the joint because it stretches, and the adhesive side dries out. The best tape, used by professionals, is brown sticky tape, which shrinks slightly, thus bringing the parts even tighter together. It should be stuck on at as close to a right angle to the break as possible; take care as you stick it on that the joint is not slipping out of alignment, and try to keep the two pieces as tightly pressed together as possible. If the piece is not too large, put it in the oven for about an hour to speed up the drying of the Araldite; have a tray underneath (preferably asbestos), and keep the temperature very low. There is just the slightest risk with this process; if the temperature is too high, the china may shatter, and the Araldite may leave a noticeable dark mark.

It is sometimes possible to glue a crack to secure it and prevent its going further, but it's an alarming process and suitable only for those with steady nerves. China does have a certain amount of elasticity, so it is possible to open the crack just a bit wider and to insert a razor blade, which will hold it open while you get some glue in. Tape it with sticky brown tape in the same way as for a break.

Small cracks can sometimes be bleached out, although great patience is needed. Once I soaked a piece in bleach for ages to no avail, and gave it up as a bad job and abandoned the piece—but when I looked at it about two weeks later, the crack had become almost invisible. Obviously, bleach can have a delayed action.

It is also possible to make a considerable improvement on pottery that has become stained a yellow or gray all the way through—coarse Staffordshire pottery is particularly prone to this. A long soak in an ordinary household bleach solution can have the almost magical effect of pushing the stain right out and returning the china to gleaming whiteness (it takes time, however, and some spots may need concentrated bleach on them).

At this stage it is worth mentioning a pernicious phenomenon of china. I have put what appears to be a perfect but dirty piece into the dishwater—and hair cracks have suddenly sprung to life. Presumably there was already stress under the glaze, and the water somehow penetrated. Now I always wipe china over with a damp cloth and only put it into water if there is no sign of cracking.

If there is a chip or a bit missing, you can do quite a reasonable repair at home; the results won't be invisible, but your work will look good enough from a distance and may rescue a beloved article. What is used for modeling depends as much as anything on the extent of the owner's search for the material, since some are specialized and difficult to find.

Putty is the substance most likely to be in a home already. It is not very good but will do a passable repair; let it dry out well and allow for shrinkage.

Barbola paste is the best all-purpose modeling material, as it is easy to use and dries fairly hard with little shrinkage. Artists' supply shops usually sell it.

Bondapaste is similar to Barbola paste, but it dries more quickly.

Araldite mixed with powders can make an excellent filler, although it's a bit messy to use (you're likely to have to make a backing of plasticine and build it up inside this, whereas the first three pastes can be built up by themselves). The best powder is titanium dioxide, which gives a white color that approximates quite well the color of unglazed china.

This mixture is very useful for repairing a break that is also slightly chipped, because it does the sticking and filling in the same step.

The first three fillers will not stay securely (partly because of slight shrinkage), and it is usually best to take the modeled piece off when it has dried and stick it back on with Araldite.

There are two good ranges of paint, Cryla and Darwi. Getting the right color and gloss is a matter of experiment, made easier by the knowledge that mistakes can be wiped off with turpentine. The Darwi varnish is good for giving a glazed finish. If these two brands are not available, ordinary oil paint will do quite a good job; if you cannot buy a clear varnish, use clear nail polish.

10 Glass

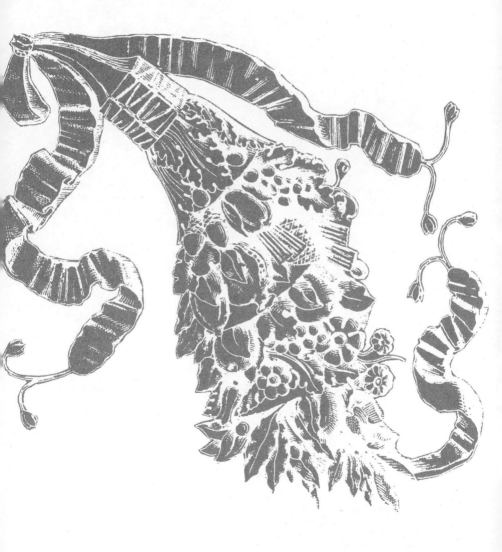

Glass is made basically from sand heated with lime and soda. Other things can be added to give special properties: lead salts make it stronger and brighter; borax makes the heatproof "Pyrex" type. The manufacture can affect performance of glass; if it has not been properly annealed (given a controlled heat treatment to release stresses), it will "fly"—develop cracks for no apparent reason. Sunlight, smoke, or heat could prompt the glass to fly.

Breakage is obviously the most common damage to glass, but most people don't realize that glass isn't the inert material it appears to be. It can crystallize, thereby becoming delicate and losing its clarity. It can change chemically when carbon dioxide in moisture reacts with a substance in the glass to form sodium carbonate and calcium silicate. This happens only over a very long period of time and is, in fact, considered a desirable patination when it gives the lovely iridescence seen, for example, on Roman glass. It is possible to remove it by a very long soaking in several bowls of distilled water, followed by a celluloid varnish, but normally it can be left on as an asset.

Perhaps more surprisingly, glass is absorbent and slightly soluble in water. This fact explains damage that sometimes puzzles people. If glass is stored in paper, for instance, for some length of time, it can absorb dye or acid from the paper; even if the paper is acid-free, there appears to be some preparation in the size that affects the glass and discolors it slightly.

The most common deterioration of glass in the home is seen on containers of liquid—decanters and flower vases, for examples. The clouding or staining that develops is thought of simply as a surface marking, removable, like silver tarnish, with a bit of abrasive. But the damage is more complex. Liquid will have very slightly dissolved the glass, which will have reacted very slightly with substances in the liquid: with lime in ordinary water, with lime and other salts in flower water, and with tartrates in wine. The result is not just a deposit, but a penetration into the glass, so that the whole surface is chemically changed; this top layer of altered glass has to be removed before a clear layer of glass will be revealed again.

So, although everyone has his pet theories about removing stains, some methods can do more harm than good. The problem is that the only sure way of removing the stain is to eat the stained glass layer away with acid, a dangerous operation that should only be done by an expert glass restorer. If another substance has already been tried and the restorer does not know about it, there is a possibility that the acid and other substance will react together to ruin the glass. I have seen this happen to a valuable piece, and it was very sad. When you try any home recipe, keep a note of it, just in case.

I have heard of ammonia being used with success. Vinegar, a weak acid, should have some effect. The ball bearing recipe, so often recommended, requires your being able to obtain ball bearings. Sand will also have the effect of wearing off the discolored layer. Whatever you do, ignore a recipe for using hydrofluoric acid—both liquid and *vapour* cause terrible burns. For stain removal by acid, send the glass to a specialist.

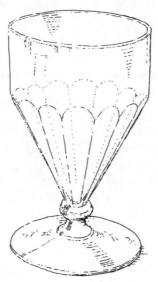

Flint Crystal Goblet

The best home method of all is to rub the stain with a fine abrasive. Accessibility is the key here. If the neck of the container is very narrow, there may be no way of reaching the mark to apply pressure; however, it may be possible to get a wooden stick with a cloth wrapped around the end inside. If this is so, dab the cloth in pumice powder and rub, finishing off with jeweler's rouge, which is a much finer abrasive. It's quite hard work but worthwhile.

Don't try rubbing with a kitchen scouring powder, because you will only create more scratches, not eliminate them. However, proprietary metal polishes are very good for both cleaning and polishing glass (they're particularly good for mirrors) .

Breaks and cracks can be mended only with rivets or glue. Rivets are so unsightly that they are used only when someone is determined to continue using an article; since rivets were the standard method of repair before the invention of super hard glues like Araldite, the problem nowadays is likely to be their removal. This is a tricky operation but possible, and the holes can, to a certain extent, be masked by fiber glass (the best glass substitute yet invented).

For gluing breaks, the expert uses industrial Araldite, applying heat, and the results can be nearly invisible, particularly where there is a natural indentation in the article (a foot can be attached to a wine glass stem, for instance, and be virtually undetectable). If you're doing a home repair, use the finest smear of Araldite, and hold the article together with brown sticky paper tape cut in strips and stretched across the joint as tightly as possible. Stand the article in a way that puts the least strain on the joint; use a tray of sand or sawdust if necessary.

Chips can always be ground out, and in fact, if they are on an accessible part of the glass (for example, around a rim), the local glass shop might be able to do it for you. The grinding is done on a hard wheel, which unfortunately is unadaptable and can't reach into curves or hollows; so anything awkward needs to be done by an expert, who will cut out a carborundum wheel to fit the pattern exactly. Similarly, a good piece should be worked on by an expert, rather than the local shop, as there is more to good grinding than just holding the object against the wheel; the edge also has to be polished, and, on a proper job, three different wheels will probably be used together.

When faced with a chip on a cheap piece and pressed for time to take it to the grinder's, I have managed to do a fair amount of smoothing by using a file with oil and finishing with jeweler's rouge. But this is a hazardous process, and I take no responsibility for anyone's trying it.

In all grinding, and indeed in all glass repair, there is an element of risk; through no fault of the repairer the piece may shatter. So, before leaving a piece, accept the possibility of a break.

It is not possible to weld a new piece of glass onto lead glass, because heat will melt the lead and cause the whole glass to go gray and cloudy. But welding is possible on soda glass. A new handle or spout could be blown and fixed on while it is molten; then it can be ground to shape.

If a piece is missing from a lead glass article, a new one could be made and glued in, but since the expense of tailor-making a piece of glass is enormous, this is not often done. And of course whole articles can be made to order, but here you're really talking money. In each case a plaster cast has to be made of the original; then a wooden mold is made; then the glass has to be blown in, cut, and polished. Cutting a pattern by hand is a very long process—just look at an average wine glass and imagine every line being cut out on one wheel and polished on another. I have seen a new decanter being made to match two others in a tantalus, and I could well understand why it was going to cost over $80.

It is also possible to have ruby glass made, but here it's not just the manufacture, but also the ingredients, that make up the cost; solid gold is thrown into the molten glass to make the real ruby color (which is why the old glass brings a good price in the antique trade today).

A search for decanter stoppers can be simplified by the knowledge that stoppers can be ground down to fit the neck of the bottle; antique shops sometimes have a store. There is a variety of methods offered for removing stuck stoppers—tapping with another piece of glass, soaking alternately in hot and cold water, soaking in oil. I think the most important requirement is patience—the stopper will eventually come out, but there is no point in forcing the issue and breaking either stopper or bottle. The most efficacious mixture is glycerine, alcohol and salt, but if these are not available, try cooking oil and alcohol. When the stopper has been soaking for several hours, wiggle it gently from side to side all the way around; prepare for it to come out with a plop without any advance easing.

Any sort of engraving can be done—in fact, there is quite a revival in the craft. Again, cost acknowledges the expense of craftsmanship today—allow thirty to forty cents each for small letters.

11 Clocks and Watches

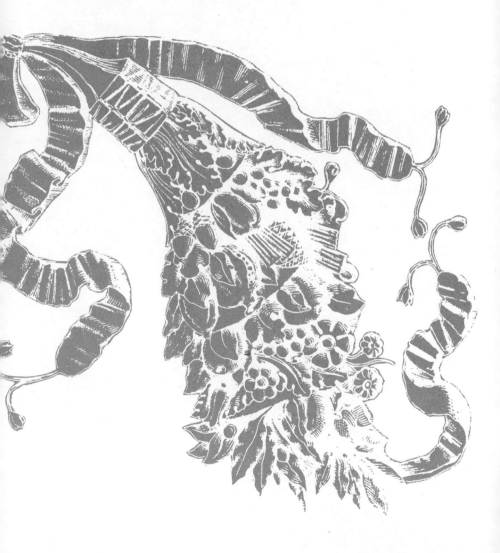

There is only one piece of advice about watches and clocks, "Never try to do anything to them yourself!" That was Leon Appleby of A. Lee, in Clerkenwell, London, a clock and watch expert with a rare enthusiasm and affection for his work.

And I remember a horrible moment when I decided to investigate a slipping clock spring myself; slowly I worked inward, unscrewing smaller and smaller screws, until the last one slipped out, and suddenly the whole works shot in the air like a jack-in-the-box, and a myriad of tiny parts fell all over the room in a shower. However, two of my scientifically minded friends have taught themselves to mend clocks. I think if you have a patient nature and an aptitude for mechanics, and if the clock is cheap and basic, then it is just possible to try it.

That main rule apart, Mr. Appleby has some very helpful general advice. When you can't see the innards, and wouldn't understand them if you could, a certain amount of guesswork about their condition is involved.

Victorian Carriage Clock

In the first instance, tip a pendulum clock from side to side—if it starts ticking, if only for a few seconds, the parts are probably all there. If the clock has a balance, twist it gently to hear the all-important ticking. If you have a key, try winding gently. If there is no clicking sound, stop immediately, as the key might kick back and hurt your hand. If you can hear a normal clicking sound as you start turning but it suddenly seems to slip, again stop right away, this time to protect the clock—the spring has become detached, and any further winding could cause considerable damage. Always stop winding if you feel any definite resistance.

Turn the hands gently to see if they are connected. The presence of an hour or an hour and half hour striking mechanism will be shown by a second winding hole, and a quarter hour striking mechanism, by a third hole; turn the hands to the striking time to find if it is working. Always let it strike the full amount before moving on, and never turn the hands backward on a striking or alarm clock.

A vital component of a clock is oil, but it is no use sloshing a little machine oil on when the clock isn't working very well. When the oil has dried out, it will have formed a hard crust mixed with dirt; if you apply new oil without proper cleaning, the abrasive dirt is still there to do its damage. Just as a car needs to be serviced and have its oil changed, so a clock needs regular attention to keep it running smoothly. Mr. Appleby recommends that a cleaning and reoiling should be carried out on a French clock every three years, and on the other, mainly larger varieties (including grandfather clocks), every five years.

To go into details of different kinds of movements will only cause confusion, but the basic ones can be recognized quite easily. The pendulum movement in clocks is obvious, and it is the one that suffers most from mishandling; people tend to carry the clock around with the pendulum still in, and the spring, a delicate piece to which the pendulum is attached, inevitably breaks. Fortunately, repair is not too expensive.

Setting a pendulum clock is tricky but important; the clock must run smoothly, with the tick as loud as the tock and the intervals between them quite even. If the ticking is uneven, lift one side or the other of the clock until it becomes even; then gently bend the crutch (Fig. 32) in the direction of the side that is raised. Replace the clock, and if the tick is still uneven but less pronounced, bend the crutch a shade more. If, however, you now have to tip the other side of the clock to obtain an even beat, the crutch has been bent too far, and it must now be bent back slightly. Always take care to make these adjustments a little at a time, as the amount of correction required is generally small.

When lifting a pendulum clock down, you can leave the pendulum in, providing you slope the clock forward ten or fifteen degrees so that the pendulum is resting against the

movement; straighten up the clock gently as you put it down
so that the pendulum is running free again. Needless to say,
the pendulum should come off if the clock is to be moved any
distance, and the crutch should have something packed
around it to keep it from wiggling.

A mercury pendulum is specially made so that changes in
temperature will not affect the running of the clock (ordinar-
ily, heat makes metal expand, and the clock slows down
slightly, while cold does the opposite). Mercury pendulums
are usually self-setting to swing in the right rhythm, and no
more than a slight push is needed to set it going; give it a
good swing, and it will settle itself down to the right level
(for mercury replacement, see *Barometers,* page 151). Other
pendulum clocks have screws that move the bob up and
down to alter the running; move the bob up to make it faster,
and down to make it slower.

The fusee movement in both clocks and watches has a sort
of miniature bicycle chain visible (Fig. 33). Make sure this
is intact, as repair or replacement is expensive. Always test
the winding mechanism; if you can turn the key both ways,
a very expensive repair is indicated.

Grandfather clocks can suffer from a peculiar disturb-
ance that is not apparent. The heavy pendulum sets up a minute rocking movement of the case itself, rather as a platoon
of soldiers crossing a bridge in time can start the bridge rocking. As the weights come down, they can be affected by this
movement, being swayed sufficiently to hit the pendulum
and stop the clock. To keep this from happening, make sure
a grandfather clock is always hard against a straight surface
or, even better, secured to the wall.

The visible parts of a clock can also suffer damage. Dials
are made generally of silvered brass (particularly on grandfather clocks), enamel, china, or painted metal. Resilvering
is quite a lengthy process, as the silver is dabbed on in a
powder form, not just painted over. Moreover, the numerals

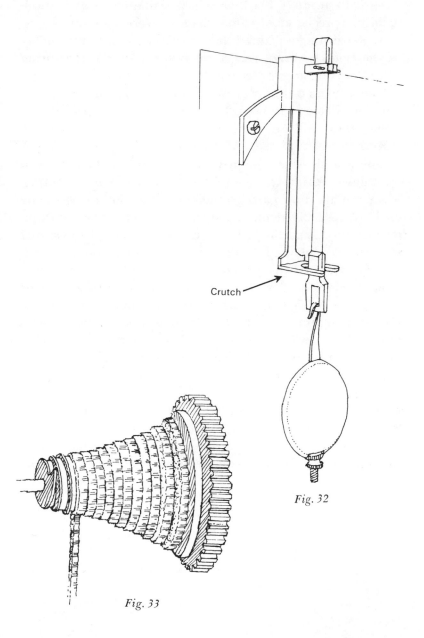

Crutch

Fig. 32

Fig. 33

are usually made of black wax in indentations, and refilling them is a precise art. Enamel dials are very expensive to repair. Repainting a painted dial, however, is quite reasonable (if the clock is cheap, you could possibly do the repainting yourself, using an enamel paint such as Valspar).

Hands on an ordinary clock will not be difficult to replace, but a good clock will often have had hands cut especially for it, and these will obviously be an expensive replacement.

Keys can be replaced quite easily.

Unless a clock is violently misused, and as long as it is overhauled regularly, there is little to make it go wrong. Wear can affect all parts of the clock, but the spring, being made of specially tempered steel and subjected to continuous bending, is particularly vulnerable. However, the spring is never particularly difficult to replace. The pivots and bearings can wear down unevenly, and this will affect the running of the clock. Sometimes the pivots and bearings can be recut to an even shape; otherwise, they must be replaced. Overwinding is a load of baloney, used by watchmakers who can't give an exact diagnosis (rather as a garage mechanic says the plugs have gone when they haven't the faintest idea what's wrong with your car) ; a normal spring would be too strong for physical pressure to break it. The spring might be in such a weak state that the next wind will break it, but that is just part of normal wear.

I have referred to "clocks" all the way through this chapter for simplicity, but the same general rules apply also to watches.

12 Barometers

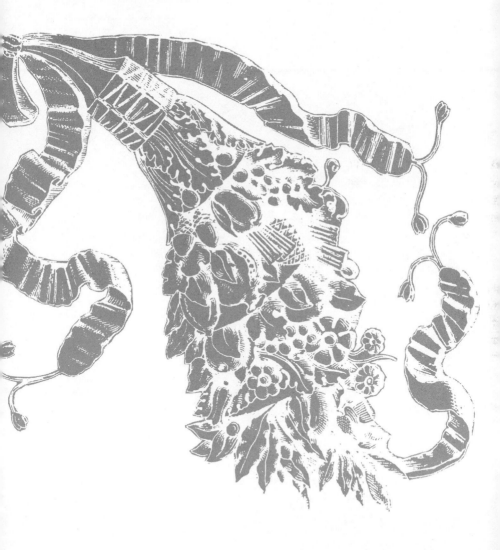

Barometers will nearly always need attention because a secure-looking case hides a fairly delicate mechanism inside, and treatment tends to be rougher than they can stand.

The principle on which a barometer operates is quite simple—a column of mercury is enclosed in the bore of a 33½ in. tube. The top end of the tube is sealed, and the bottom is open and exposed to air pressure. Between the mercury and the sealed end is a vacuum allowing the variation of air pressure to push the mercury up and down the bore of the tube.

Although there are some unusual (and valuable) barometers around, the air pressure change has been shown in two basic ways for about 200 years. In a "stick" barometer, the actual level of mercury is seen against a scale; here the tube will end in a "cistern," which will be either glass or boxwood (Fig. 34). In a "wheel," or "banjo" barometer, there are two weights joined by a cotton thread that runs over a pulley wheel; one weight enters the end of the tube to be activated

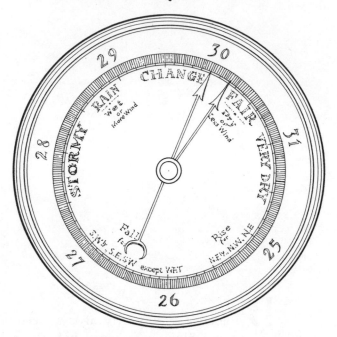

by the mercury level, and the other is a balance weight. As the wheel is turned by the changing level of mercury, it rotates a pointer on the front of the dial (Fig. 35).

In the middle of the last century a neater method, which did away with mercury, was found for showing the change in air pressure; here the air presses onto a vacuum sealed into a round metal container (Fig. 36). Known as an "aneroid" barometer, this is not necessarily more accurate than the mercury variety; it is just smaller and tidier.

With mercury barometers, inevitably at some stage the vacuum inside the tube goes, and the pressure cannot activate the mercury properly. Boxwood cisterns are a particularly weak point because they have bags at the bottom that can tear easily. Once there is a gap, dirt gets into the mercury, air bubbles are trapped, and usually a new tube has to be put in (it would not even be worth the expense of refining the old mercury).

Fig. 34

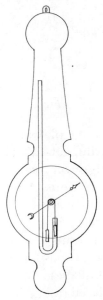

Fig. 35

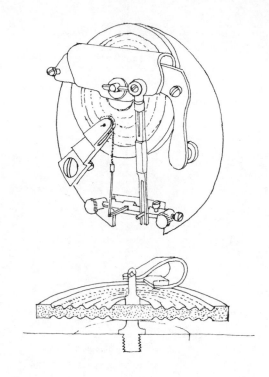

Fig. 36

Whatever you do, don't play around with the mercury or try to refill the tube yourself—it's poisonous, and if you put a finger in your mouth or on food after touching a drop, the consequences could be serious. Anyway, it's not worth trying to buy mercury yourself—you would only pay more than you should at the drugstore.

There are wholesale firms doing complete barometer repairs. Here not only are tubes replaced (or made to order if they are an awkward shape), but every other part of the barometer can be replaced, too. All the bezels, thermometers, little mirrors, hands, and faces can be found completely in period (they make new barometers as well) ; because barometers of all ages tend to be standard in shape and size, it is usually not much of a problem to find the right replacement. They also have woodworkers to restore the case. Generally, however, their services are only available through a retailer (Marshall Field and Company, Chicago, for instance), so take your barometer into the nearest clock, watch, or camera shop.

Dials are usually silvered in the same way as grandfather clock faces, with a silver powder being dabbed on by hand. It's a more complicated and skilled job than the description makes it sound, but nevertheless it's not difficult to have it redone. If the mercury has leaked out of the tube, small droplets may well have eaten into the dial, so you may need a new dial, not just resilvering. Mercury fortunately does not affect the wood. Numbers and figures are also applied to a barometer face in the same way as it is in a grandfather clock: black wax is filled into etched designs. Again, it is not difficult to have these rewaxed if they have become faint.

Many barometers are damaged by being moved. Wheel barometers should have a plug that can be inserted into the end of the tube to prevent the escape of mercury, but inevitably these plugs are missing; see if a local barometer retailer can obtain one for you if the barometer is due to be transported. Stick barometers should be kept upright and steady.

13 Cylinder Music Boxes

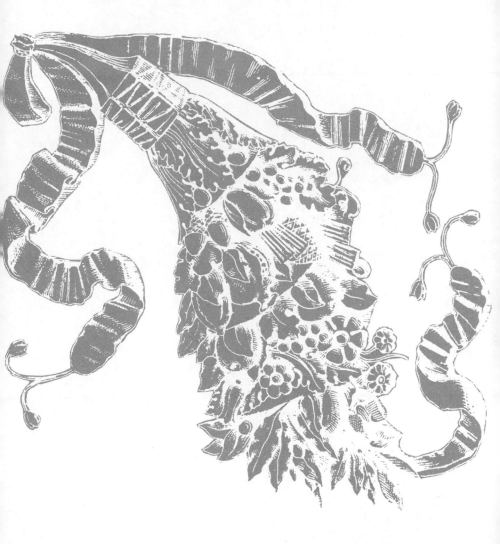

Cylinder music boxes often turn up in attics, where they were thrown in disgust when the gramophone was invented. But now, with their increase in value, they are being lovingly carried down again. The first reaction of a person who finds one is to wind it up and play it. But DON'T —this could be fatal. The spring may still have power, but it may not be connected properly; when you release the spring, the cylinder may start whizzing round at far too great a speed, breaking both the pins on the cylinder and the teeth of the comb. At the end of its gyration, it may also break the "governor," which has an endless screw that is the center of the winding power. Moreover, it may kick back and hurt your hand (see Fig. 37 for various parts).

Turn the cylinder by hand to listen, until an expert can have a look to tell you that everything is all right.

If you are contemplating the purchase of a musical box, be sure that all the tunes are there; when pins have become too damaged for rescue, sometimes a whole tune is taken off. When the box is playing, keep it standing steady and don't knock it, or the teeth may hit the pins and cause damage.

Bent pins can be straightened, but this is really a job for an expert; some will inevitably be broken in the process, even

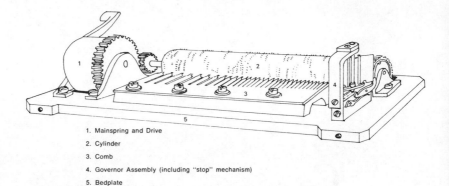

1. Mainspring and Drive
2. Cylinder
3. Comb
4. Governor Assembly (including "stop" mechanism)
5. Bedplate

Fig. 37

with expert handling. Broken pins, however, can be mended only in Switzerland, which is obviously a very expensive procedure; more than that, it is a very long job—the last I heard, the delay was two years.

Other than that, all broken parts can either be replaced or mended in this country. Sometimes another box is cannibalized to provide parts; otherwise the pieces have to be cut (no two music boxes are exactly alike). As Graham Webb, one of the biggest dealers in music boxes, said, "You have to be a bit of blacksmith in this business." The comb teeth are most likely to need attention, and here the repair, although tricky and tedious, is not as difficult as it might appear.

Dealers are probably too busy with their own work to take on much outside repair, but they will offer sympathetic help. And for anyone with a mechanical turn of mind, Graham Webb's book *The Cylinder Musical Handbook* gives all the practical details of repairing and cleaning every part, with clear enough instructions for the amateur to follow.

14 Carpets and Materials

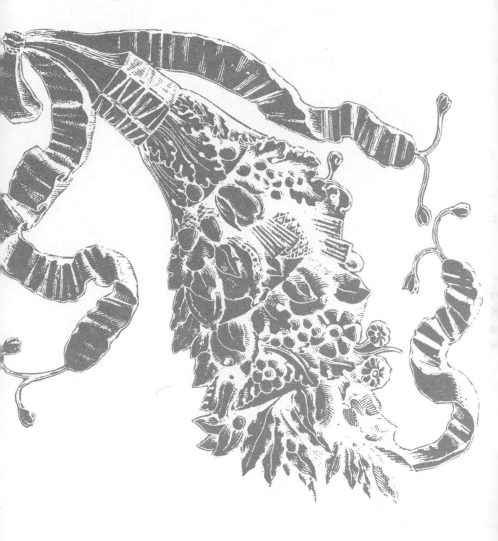

Turkish and Persian carpets were something of a revelation to me. Some look magnificent, but some look very dull—and yet they are worth a lot of money. Even rugs that look as if they might be relegated to a kitchen may turn out to be worth a great deal of money. And silk, which is the most desirable material, sometimes doesn't look like silk at all. So be very careful what you get rid of if you ever have to clear a house—just in case.

It's a nice thought that, once you have sorted out what's what, you could lay an investment on the floor. Very simply, even the best Axminster or Wilton will start to depreciate as soon as you lay it down, whereas a good Oriental carpet will always increase in value.

Most of the carpets you see around are likely to be of nineteenth century manufacture, but still handmade with silk or wool threads tied in with millions of knots. Obviously it is very important to prevent any warp or weft threads from breaking, or an awful lot of carpet could start unraveling. For a start, a carpet should be laid correctly, and this method was described to me by an expert cleaner and renovator.

163

If you put a woven Oriental carpet, which is comparatively thin, on top of a pile carpet like Axminster, and watch what happens when pressure is brought down on the two, you can see that the Oriental carpet "rides" on the other—it makes a definite sideways movement. Multiply this by a number of footsteps, and it's easy to see that the carpet ends up with a lot of pushing and pulling, which will eventually move it to one side of the room, depending on the angle of the pile underneath. Eventually, too, something somewhere will be broken.

The only way to avoid this is to make a well in the carpet or an underlay underneath and fit the Oriental carpet inside. Use a thin underlay in the well—if it is too thick, heels will dig through the carpet to it.

The cleaning expert juggles potions for treating stains with the pleasure of a wizard concocting spells. Each stain requires judging separately, so it is impossible to lay down rules for comprehensive treatment. However, here are some general hints (which apply to all kinds of carpets, not just the Oriental variety).

It is most important not to let the back become soaked because the threads may open up and loosen the knots. Bissell rug shampoo is best for general cleaning, and Picrin is good for stain removal.

A bucket of white sawdust (which a butcher might obtain for you) is very useful as a standby for accidents; it draws the stain up and if applied in time can sometimes eliminate it altogether without any further treatment (an expert once rescued a coffee-soaked carpet by sprinkling rug shampoo and sawdust—when the sawdust was swept up 24 hours later, there was no sign of a stain). If you have no sawdust, starch will act the same way.

For greasy stains, good first aid is a liberal sprinkling of talcum powder, which will sometimes soak them up entirely if applied in time. For specific stains consult an expert and always take great care if the carpet is valuable. For general treatment, oil of pine is a volatile solvent that breaks down many stains; it should be kept in a dark, well-stoppered bottle, or sticky resins may form which will themselves damage fabrics.

Whenever you clean a carpet, make quite sure the pile is brushed back the right way. This is more difficult than might appear—even an expert sometimes takes five minutes to determine the direction.

Gros Point Victorian Footstool

All antique textile cleaning should be approached with extreme caution. I once immersed a nice Victorian sampler into soapflakes and swished it around, only to find that my hands were holding nothing but a few threads. Ideally, you should rest the material on a piece of polythene and cover gently with warm water, lifting it out again equally gently. If the material is openwork (for example lace), tack it on to the polythene sheet first. If the colors look as though they might run, fix them with a 5% solution of either common salt or acetic acid. The water for washing should be either rain water or distilled water, and the best soap is a saponin, which comes from the higher plants and is much gentler than detergents (it also lathers easily and removes oil by forming an emulsion with it).

If there is a grease stain, put the material face down on top of blotting paper, with, ideally, a sheet of glass underneath; apply the antidote with an eye dropper from the back, circling the stain first and working inward so that the stain doesn't spread.

When mounting material don't use iron nails, as rust will react with sulfur dioxide in the air and will eventually become iron sulfate, which will rot the fabric through the subsequent production of sulfuric acid. Copper tacks are best. And cover the back well to prevent dust and dirt from entering.

A new development, very useful for needlework in poor condition, is mounting on nylon gauze. In the case of a sampler, for instance, with some moth holes and tears, this can make the sampler secure and the defects almost invisible.

15 Gilding

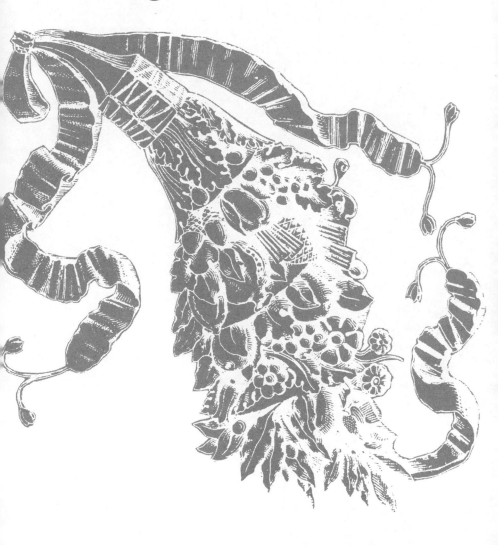

Gilding wood is an immensely painstaking and complicated process—and, naturally, an expensive one. However, if the piece of furniture is valuable enough, the money spent is obviously well justified. And if you are an excellent handyman, you can turn a set of ordinary beech or elm chairs into something splendid.

The basis of water gilding (the best and most commonly found on furniture) is gesso, a mixture of well washed chalk (whitening) and rabbit skin glue (size), applied in several layers. Although it is possible to give a textbook recipe (equal parts of whiting, glue, water, and zinc white), knowing the right mix comes from experience, not measuring; because the quality of the ingredients can vary, there is no hard and fast rule, just a feel for the right combination.

Certainly, if the mix is wrong, the gesso can be too hard to work on properly, or it will break up and crumble. The deterioration may not show up immediately, but only over a period of time, and the whole gilding may be ruined.

On ornate parts of the wood, the gesso will have to be

carved to bring out the detail. Then the whole is covered with gold size, which is clay and comes in three basic colors: yellow, red, and blue (white is also available but not generally used on this type of gilding).

The size causes more confusion about gilding than does anything else. Because the gold leaf is only ¼ of 1,000th of an inch thick, it wears down quite easily, and the size shows through. Because red is the color most commonly used, to the uninitiated it appears that the gold itself has tarnished into a strange color.

There is a sad tale that illustrates this dilemma. An expert gilded a table for a wealthy woman, who, on its return, placed a vase of flowers on top. Some water dripped down, the maid mopped up the water, rubbed too fiercely, and showed up the same red size underneath; the mistress of the house ordered more rubbing to remove the "tarnish," whereupon the maid took the cloth through to the gesso. The owner brought the table back in to the expert with complaints that the job hadn't been properly done!

The gold leaf is applied in what appears to be a primitive and haphazard method. A soft brush is rubbed against the cheek and picks up enough static electricity to make a leaf stick to it. The leaf is then dabbed onto wet size. It is not smoothed down until the whole area has been covered and is dry; then what looks like a mess of leaf edges is smoothed rapidly down. Putting on just enough gold leaf to cover the area without having to touch in any gaps, but not so much that leaf is wasted unnecessarily, is an accomplished art.

Water gilding comes out looking mat, and the highlights are then polished with a variety of agate tools (these improve with age, so a gilder will prize his own highly). Another kind of gilding, with a base of oil size, is also practiced, but it has a different appearance and tends to be shinier than water gilding. An agate burnisher cannot be used on it, so the brightness has to be controlled during the application by

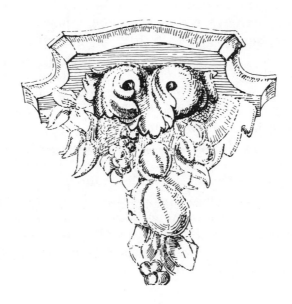

Carved and Gilded Bracket

the quality of the size and the degree of "tack" (or stickiness) when the leaf is actually being dabbed on. The shape of the article will likewise affect the brightness—curved surfaces reflect more light than flat ones and so appear brighter. Generally, oil gilding is likely to be found on painted surfaces or outdoor work—railings, coats of arms, and so on.

The gold layer is a protective medium in itself, but because it is so thin, great care must be taken not to diminish it in any way. Water is the great enemy of water gilding. If the gold has worn sufficiently to let it in from the top, it will dissolve the size. If it reaches the gesso, you're really in trouble—the gesso can easily crumble, and then the whole gilding disintegrates.

It's not just a matter of avoiding water directly. Moisture can cause damage, but in a more insidious way. A gilded mirror hanging on a damp wall, for instance, might look all right from the front for years; but behind, moisture is working its way into the gesso, which is slowly disintegrating, so that when the day comes to take the mirror down from the wall, the gilding will just drop off. Or the wood might expand from damp sufficiently to crack the gesso. And, of course, central heating can have the bad effect of drying the wood so that it shrinks and cracks the gesso.

Whatever you do when faced with damaged gilding, *don't patch it up with gold paint*. It has to be removed with a chemical stripper, which has to be "killed," and the media used for "killing" the stripper, because it is a spirit, is as injurious to gold leaf as is water. Moreover, some of the particles of metal that make up the "gold" paint remain in the surface of the gold and are extremely difficult to remove.

If any touching up has to be done, imitate the size underneath, not the gold; this can be done using ocher and umber water paints for red size or other water paints, depending on the color of the size.

Since gilding is such a long and expensive process, there are naturally short cuts practiced. Spraying with gold paint is one, but this has a harsh look compared with gold leaf. A long established substitute for gold leaf is "Dutch metal," a very clever artificial gold made from copper and brass and used for several hundred years. In fact, applying it by the water gilding method takes longer than gold leaf, but the raw materials cost less. It is satisfactory on oil size, but in most cases it debases the value of the article. So if you're having something gilded, make sure that real gold is used.

A sensible suggestion to anyone looking for a reliable gilder is to ask a gold leaf manufacturer for names.

16 Dolls

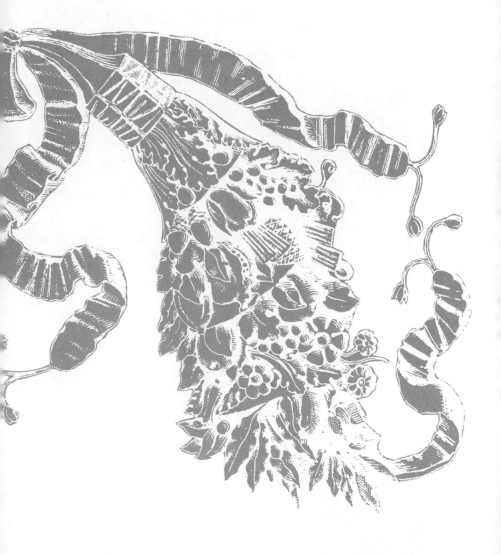

Dolls, being playthings, understandably hardly ever remain in perfect condition (except perhaps for those superb late nineteenth century wax dolls that were not subjected to nursery rough and tumble in the usual way). In whatever condition you find a doll, the specialist dealers make one passionate plea—*do not use Araldite to stick either wig or limbs back on.* You will make the process of restoring very much more difficult. Moreover, you might even miss a sale. One dealer points out that the condition of the top part of the head vitally affects the value of the doll, and if she can't lift the wig off to see if it is broken or not, she won't even contemplate buying it. And as far as the limbs go, because the body is invariably made up of a cardboard "composition," and Araldite is virtually insoluble, a glued limb has to be ripped off before restoration can start.

Dolls' hospitals immediately spring to mind for doll repairs. But these are rather misleading places. Usually, they can only repair *modern* dolls, replacing limbs or eyes and fitting modern nylon wigs. So choose the "hospital" with care, making sure they understand old dolls and ask, perhaps, to see work in progress as a final check. Otherwise, ask doll dealers for their advice—they might be able to put you in touch with a restorer in your area. Or they will always give you advice about restoring the doll yourself.

The majority of dolls around are of nineteenth and twentieth century German manufacture, with beautiful bisque heads attached to wood or composition bodies (with feet and hands sometimes of bisque and china). As you can see from the illustration (Fig. 38), the limbs are joined by elastic—in this case, a special round stringing elastic—while the head has a round wooden dome at the bottom from which elastic joins to the legs. The head usually has a cardboard "lid" and a gauze-based wig (Fig. 39).

There are plenty of points for breakage, and this makes home mending difficult. Sometimes the elastic is pulled too tight and splits the body, or eyes that have become detached from the bridge (Fig. 40) are stuck back directly into the sockets. Sometimes wrong heads have been replaced on bodies (for example, a baby's head on a girl's body). Childhood play also leaves its legacy of breaks and cracks.

If the head is damaged, there is really no point in trying to salvage the doll, as anything other than an expert repair will look awful, and an expert repair could well cost more than the value of the doll. The only exception would be a doll so rare that it's worth preserving—and only a doll expert could tell you that. However, if the doll is of sentimental value and you would prefer to maintain it with a visible repair rather than to discard it, see the chapter on china repairs.

Moving eyes suffer from children's poking them out to see how they work. If the bridge is broken, mend it with plastic glue; a number of good brands are available.

To replace missing eyes go to an expert with a stock of spares, because the eyes must be in period (some of the

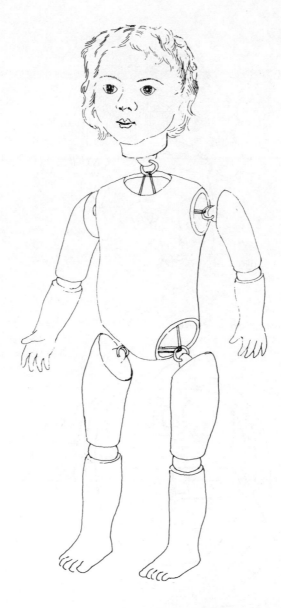

Fig. 38

Fig. 39

'Opening and closing eyes'

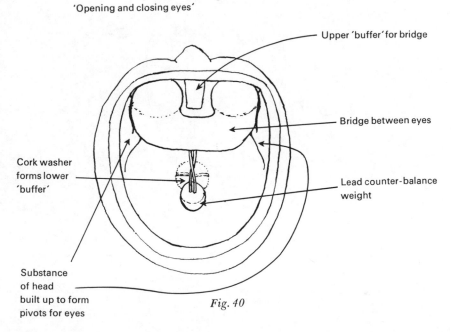

Upper 'buffer' for bridge

Bridge between eyes

Cork washer forms lower 'buffer'

Lead counter-balance weight

Substance of head built up to form pivots for eyes

Fig. 40

earliest ones were made like miniature paperweights and are very beautiful in themselves).

What you use to mend holes or splits on the body depends on where the damage is. The hardest kind of plastic padding is needed around the leg sockets. The main part of the body can take tiling cement. Barbola paste, a useful imitation china, can be used to build up fingers.

Matching up the paint is an art. The best basic paints are either Cryla or Humbrol. Cryla can be bought from specialist art shops in a huge range of colors, and fortunately the varnish variety has three grades—mat, medium, or shiny. Humbrol will more likely be found in hobby shops and is shinier than Cryla. However, the glaze can be controlled by adding talcum powder or face powder—in fact, matching a flesh color is very much a matter of trial and error, as every doll will be slightly different. To merge the new paint in, the fingertips are the best tool, messy though that is.

The head often has a wooden dome at the bottom, from which the stringing elastic goes through to the legs, and this dome is sometimes missing (see Fig. 41). A direct replace-

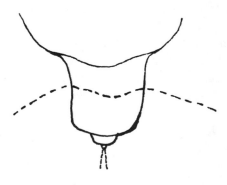

Fig. 41

ment is virtually impossible, so you must use a blazer type button, turning it upside down so that the metal loop used for sewing it onto the blazer is facing down. Try to find a wooden button of this pattern, but if this is not possible, a metal one will suffice. Line the hollow into which it will fit with kid or cardboard. Insure that the loop on the button is securely attached; if necessary stick it with Araldite. Bend a piece of wire into an S shape and hook this, with the stringing elastic, onto the button loop.

The hair is sometimes thin and very often tangled. A thin patch can sometimes be disguised by rearranging the remaining hair, adding a ribbon, or covering up even more with a hat.

If the hair is matted, *don't* comb it as you would your own (i.e., starting from the top of the scalp and just pulling the comb down). This will pull the hair out from the base. Instead, separate a small strand at the bottom (that is, around the neck), gently ease the tangles out, and work up through the wig in this way.

Doll hair is normally washable, with certain reservations. If the mount is gauze, leave it alone. The more normal canvas mounts will withstand a certain amount of wetting, but obviously the less it is soaked, the better. Use either shampoo or dishwashing liquid well diluted, and gently squeeze the hair in it; don't rub or the tangles will return. Replace the canvas back onto the head before it is completely dry so that it retains the right shape.

Giving a doll a completely new wig is unfortunately difficult. There are no suitable ready-made ones on the market, and there is a dearth of restorers prepared to make them (ask a dealer who might put you in touch with someone). It is a job that someone with nimble hands and a lot of patience could do on his own, and there is no better guide than Audrey Johnson's book *How to Repair and Dress Old Dolls*. Although she gives various possible materials, collectors I have talked to recommend mohair as the most adaptable.

Wax dolls can suffer not only from childish handling but also from the atmosphere that dries them out and cracks them. They are occasionally made from solid wax, but more often either are hollow, having been poured into a mold, or are made up of a covering of wax on a composition base. In the last case, the coloring may be either underneath the wax or on top.

If the wax is dirty, clean it in the first instance with cold cream on a piece of cotton wool. If this still leaves some dirt, add a small amount of pure turpentine, and use it very sparingly, as it softens the wax. Turpentine can sometimes smooth out small cracks on the same principle, softening the wax so that it can be pushed into the cracks, but do this with great care. The turpentine will also remove any painted features, so keep a record of them before they are obliterated; use oil paint to replace them.

Composition heads with a covering of wax can be re-dipped, but this is a more complicated operation than it seems. The new wax must be of the right color, texture, and temperature, and the head must go in at exactly the right angle and very steadily; otherwise the wax becomes ridged. Again, Audrey Johnson's book gives practical advice for doing it at home. Touching up a missing piece of wax with candle wax never works well, because the colors are too different, and in the process you are likely to mess up more of the head.

Never throw away a doll's clothes, however bad their condition; they might be a valuable guide to the date of the doll. Dressing dolls in period costume is enormous fun for anyone with a reasonable amount of patience, and a study of source material could be fascinating. Here, of course, Audrey Johnson's book is invaluable.

17 Objets d'Art and Miscellaneous

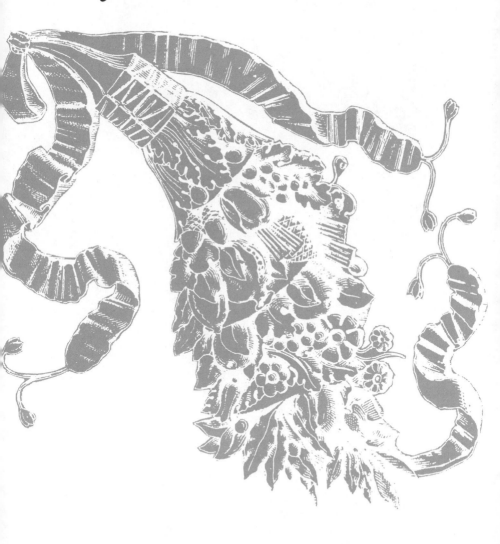

You never know when something interesting is going to turn up in the ground, whether it's in the back garden, out in the fields, or as part of a deliberate search (a friend of mine used to go to a well in a famous Roman city ruin when it had rained and find curious bits and pieces floating about). However tempting, don't try to clean anything, but keep it intact with its surrounding earth as long as possible. Archaeologists can derive information from the earth that the layman can't see—pollen grains may help date an object, for instance, or minute traces in the earth may show the type of container in which it was held. Don't change the temperature too drastically—for instance, by drying something wet in an oven. And, of course, don't use any cleaning powders or preparations.

Take the find to the nearest museum, where they will probably be only too glad to give interested advice; if that fails, take it to a museum that specializes in archaeological finds. Many large museums have restoration departments that will give advice about cleaning and preserving.

Cutlery

The handles of cutlery have frequently become loose and discolored. Most are fixed to the blades with pitch, which is poured in molten and sets hard. Unfortunately, it is very hard to buy pitch, but usually there is enough left inside the handle to refix the blade; if there is not, either plastic padding or Araldite can be used.

To take the handle off you must melt the remaining pitch, and this presents a problem: the pitch must be heated without damaging the handle. How you do this depends on your patience and the risks you are prepared to take. The best way is to hold the joint between the blade and handle with tongs in the steam of a boiling kettle spout, which directs the heat where it is needed. Less tedious is to balance the cutlery over a small saucepan of boiling water (use a non-culinary saucepan, as pitch may drip into it). If you use this method, check carefully to determine whether the handles are ivorine (plastic) or ivory. I have never forgotten leaving a bundle on top of the gas stove while I went into the sitting room; a few minutes later I noticed a red glow coming from the kitchen and went back to find the whole thing on fire. The handles were ivorine, which had caught fire and turned into a charred heap. Even if the handles are ivory, keep the jet low and the handles well away, as fire will do no good to ivory either.

The quickest way to melt the pitch is to immerse the cutlery into boiling water, but this softens and warps ivorine handles (although they can be bent back into shape) and is harsh on ivory.

However you heat the cutlery, try to push the handle back on firmly when the pitch inside has just melted, not when it has started to ooze out; otherwise there may not be enough pitch left inside to hold the handle.

If some handles in a set are missing or split, it is worth searching through stores or rummage sales for replacements.

Desk Boxes

These lovely pieces of furniture, many of them Regency, have come into their own now, although I think they are still inexpensive. Often the hinges have been broken or are missing, and unfortunately they cannot always be replaced. The ones shaped like a T-square are not made anymore, and

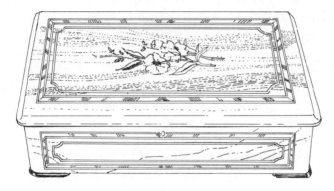

Inlaid Music Box

the narrow ones that fold completely flat, with a bit protruding from the back of the box, are only made in a limited number of sizes now. If the baize or leather inside has rubbed right through at the hinges, leaving top or bottom wooden flaps loose, the instant-sticking wide plastic in a roll makes a serviceable repair (it comes in quite a variety of colors, including not a bad imitation leather).

Enamel

Enamel, being glass, is very fragile; just see if you can find a cloisonée vase that is absolutely perfect. More botching up with paint probably goes on in this field than in any other, since paint-filled chips usually look worse than chips. Probably the only hope of a passable repair is to melt celluloid in amyl acetate, adding the appropriate oil color, but even this is not very satisfactory. Refiring new enamel is virtually impossible because the necessary heat would melt the rest of the piece.

Ivory and Ivory-Backed Brushes

There is a great difference between the creamy patina of antique ivory and yellow staining; the first is desirable and should be left, but the other can be treated. Ordinary household bleach will shift the yellow, although there are snags; immersion in liquid might open up cracks in the ivory, and the stain might reappear after a time.

Lacquer

When it comes to lacquer, the gap between the demand for the antiques and the availability of restorers has reached the almost impossible. Along with all things Oriental, demand for antique lacquer is booming, but there are very few people who are really skilled at restoring it.

However, one expert was able to pass on some information. First of all, the lacquer furniture you see will not be covered with true lacquer, which is made from the sap of a Japanese tree. It will be a paint invented in the eighteenth century to imitate the real lacquer for fashionable Orientally inclined Europeans. This paint is not made any more. What is sold as "lacquer" in shops today is only a poor approximation. So the expert has his own secret formula, learned and perfected during twenty-one years of training with Chinese and Japanese artists.

Lacquer has a base of gesso, so that, like gilding, it is prone to damage from moisture and should be kept in a carefully balanced temperature.

Marble

Marble is associated with permanence in the public's mind, because of all those ancient Greek and Roman statues, but, in fact, it's not a strong material. Technically it's an aggregate of crystals of calcite, which is a kind of high-class chalk, and much of its appeal is due to the highly polished finish it is given. It stains easily, fractures easily, and can be warped by heat or cold (it's really not very suitable for fireplaces or outdoor statues, despite tradition).

There are a couple of recipes that can be tried for stains on marble. The simplest is to make a thick paste of ordinary powder detergent, add a bit of bleach, and keep this over the spot for any amount of time up to two days (keep it moist with a cover at first). The more complicated recipe is to add equal amounts of quicklime and caustic potash to melted soap and to leave this on for several days. There are marble cleaning kits on the market today (Weiman's has one kit for badly-stained marble and another for normally dirty marble). Professional marble cleaners discourage home treatment, but you can try it if you like. Be careful not to get spirits or hair spray on a professionally polished piece of marble, as both will melt the surface polish, which then will have to be completely renewed.

If the surface is dull and you can't afford a professional polish (or if the piece is a statue), ordinary furniture wax will give a certain amount of shine and protection. Weiman's marble cleaner polishes as it cleans.

Masons will give a machine polish, if the article is transportable to them. This is quite a complicated process, involving several machines, so don't be surprised if the cost is higher than you expect. They might also smooth over chips. If the marble is to be kept outside, seal the surface with silicone.

Mirrors

Mirror glass is unfortunately expensive, and so is resilvering and beveling. In cost, there really is not much difference between having the old mirror resilvered and a new one cut.

Since not many glass cutters also do beveling, resilvering may be preferable. Hand mirrors are usually filled with pitch before the mirror is put in, and a silver rim holds the mirror in place; the pitch often breaks up into lumps from the continual handling, and jagged ends come through the silver (which is often thin anyway), and the raised parts of the silver nearly always collect dents. To reach the silver (and to take the mirror out), snap the silver rim out by prizing underneath it with a knife; the pitch can then be chipped away, and any dents in the silver can be eased out with a wooden spoon or handle. Small holes can be filled in with soft solder, but bear in mind the warning about soft solder given in the silver chapter. To replace the pitch, melt it in a saucepan (a foul-smelling operation) and pour it back into the mirror.

Mother of Pearl

Small chips can be smoothed with a fine file and then polished with jeweler's rouge. As it is a soft material, you may be lucky enough to replace missing parts yourself by buying a new piece and cutting it down; it is very tedious but can be done.

Papier Mâché

Many papier-mâché articles have small pieces missing and I must admit I simply fill these in with plastic wood, using either blackboard black or stove black to color them. To make proper papier-mâché, tear newspapers into tiny pieces, leave it to soak in water for a day, strain off the surplus water, and mix the remaining pulp with flour paste; you will probably have to stick the modeled piece on with Araldite for a secure job.

Tortoiseshell

Tortoiseshell is basically a layer of horny skin and, like living skin, the surface can dry out. Even a small amount of sunshine can do this, making the top lose its luster and turn white. Sometimes it is possible to effect rescue by replacing the oil; rub on either wax polish or linseed oil repeatedly. But more often than not, the dead layer has to be removed and the underneath layer repolished.

Use a very fine wet and dry emery paper, and work as gently and evenly as possible. When the white layer is finally off, use jeweler's rouge for polishing—either on a buffing wheel if you have one and if the object is not too delicate, or by hand. If no jeweler's rouge is obtainable, you will have to do the best you can with wax polish.

Missing pieces can be replaced, but it is a very expensive process. There is no substitute, either, that can be made to look remotely like tortoiseshell. Because it is now a very desirable material and objects made from it are much sought after, look after any you may have. Don't leave it too near heat, and don't let the sun shine directly on it.

Weapons

As with watches and clocks, the most important advice is—don't tamper with weapons. Don't try to cock a gun or push any mechanical part, as there will probably be some rust somewhere inside and you may break a part—perhaps a vital one. And, of course, don't under any circumstances try to fire an old gun, even if it looks empty of ammunition— you could do yourself lethal harm. If an old gun is wanted for use, a gunsmith will restore it and fire it in a special firing chamber to see if it is working safely; there is a certain risk that the gun will blow itself up when this is done. More or less any part can be replaced on a gun, although the replacement will affect its value. Dealers and gunsmiths always have a selection of spare parts. It is hard to make the valves tight because they are usually made of ivory or horn and absorb damp and dirt; to temper a new spring is difficult, as the tempering has to be just right—not too hard and not too soft.

18 Using Antiques

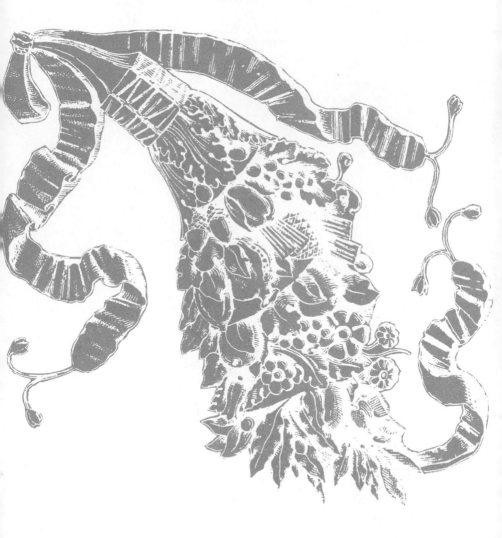

Most people are very unimaginative about antiques. In the first place, there is a mystique about them that sets them apart from the usual household furnishings; whereas a couple can go into a store and buy a new glass vase without too much soul-searching, when they look around an antique shop, a sort of inhibition sets in. In the second place, people seem to be plagued with a total conformity of usage. I once had a cylindrical brass umbrella stand and put some fire irons in it simply to get them out of the way. A man came into the shop and asked anxiously if the stand was for umbrellas or fire irons; he was most relieved when I said it was really an umbrella stand, because that's what he was looking for. But it so obviously would hold fire irons as well that it wouldn't have mattered what it was made for originally; if, however, he wanted to use it as an umbrella stand, that's what it immediately became.

Certainly, there is an eccentric flaunting of unconventional furnishing that is as annoying as the style it is desperately trying to avoid. But it should be possible to look at an object with an imaginative and unbiased eye, and to buy it on the basis of "Yes, it's nice, now what could I use it for?" There are millions of objects around, made with the kind of care and craftsmanship we shall never see again; what a shame it is that these objects don't beautify more homes.

The ideas I offer will certainly not appeal to everybody; as much as anything, they are included in order to stimulate other people to walk through shops and markets with a less prejudiced eye.

Bathroom

This always seems to be an unnessarily clinical room. The steam obviously prevents hanging the family Gainsborough there, but there is scope for a lot more luxury at not too great a cost. Victorian washing china—soap dishes, tooth-mugs, and so on—can still be bought reasonably. Old tiles can make an interesting bath or sink background. The Edwardians went in for ornate brass or wood pipe racks that could convert easily into toothbrush racks; give them a good coating of polyurethene varnish to make them as hygienic as the plastic variety. Those stag horns mounted on wooden shields would make good towel hangers, and they're still cheap to buy; again polyurethene will render them hygienic.

When it comes to bath salt and talcum powder containers, imagination can run free. There are silver-topped glass jars, old medicine jars, or even glass decanters. The decanters would be marvelous for bubble bath solution and, on the whole, because they're not very salable, they tend to be cheap. And for decoration on the walls, there is a whole range of Victorian seashell decorations—expensive in specialist "Victoriana" shops but usually cheap elsewhere. It would be interesting, for example, to build up a collection of anchors made out of seashells.

Kitchen

In my opinion, there is more scope for using antiques in the kitchen than anywhere else. So many of the old implements still work far better than modern ones—coffee grinders, pepper grinders, pestles and mortars, pastry crimpers, and so on—that a purchase hardly has to be justified at all. And it's possible to combine utility and beauty very well. Instead of those horrible plastic flour and sugar containers, use old stoneware tobacco jars—they will keep the contents fresher for longer. There are lovely spice cabinets around, and, although they are not likely to be cheap, they probably won't be much more costly than flimsy new ones. In both cases, a lining of aluminum foil will make the containers hygienic. I would be a bit dubious about using apothecary jars, in case there was still a poison vapor that survived all washing and lining, but it should be possible to get the jars medically sterilized if you're determined to use them.

A friend bought one of those lovely old mahogany medicine cupboards, with doors that swing open and shelves for the jars both behind the doors and in front. All the jars were missing, but it takes modern spice jars perfectly; now it is an attractive piece of furniture, used happily every day. Mahogany hanging shelves can also make an attractive support for spice or food jars, but unfortunately these now cost a great deal. However, ordinary deal shelves will take a mahogany stain to look quite smart.

I suppose no housewife now is prepared to use old-fashioned scales, juggling with a multitude of weights. But for anyone who can be bothered, there are some decorative ones around—although they have become fashionable and therefore costly (I think people put flower pots on them). I once saw a hanging set that had been gilded—magnificent. And gilding isn't an outrageously expensive process.

Brass and copper always give a comfortable look to a kitchen, and copper pans are the best sort for cooking. They are not easy to buy reasonably, but the old ones are usually so heavy and solid that the extra you pay compared to a modern one is usually worth it. Tinning the inside is essential, or you will get copper poisoning, but again it's not a particularly expensive process. Other than usable items, there are stacks of decorative brass and copper items around, just one of which could give an ordinary kitchen a lift. And it is sometimes possible to buy lidless copper kettles at low cost—they make good flower containers.

When it comes to keeping recipes, there are all sorts of possibilities for containers. Those domed letter boxes have now become rather expensive, but they are still worth spending money on because of the excellent craftsmanship. Empty desk or sewing boxes can be bought cheaply, and a little bit of ingenuity could turn one into a recipe filing box.

For holding bills or shopping reminders you can get really frivolous. Victorian card holders shaped like hands in brass are real works of art, and there are other letter and card holders in a wide variety of designs. If I ever have a skirt holder in stock, I have to spend hours explaining it: these are Victorian novelties that held the hem of a skirt and were fixed to the waist by a chain so that the modest young lady going up or down stairs just had to pull the chain to avoid tripping over her skirt instead of leaning down. One of these would make a practical shopping list holder.

Fruit compotes never seem to be very salable, which always surprises me, because nothing sets off a kitchen or dining area better than a magnificent dish of fruit—a luxury look for very little cost. The Victorians made some lovely ones, and, if my experience is anything to go by, they shouldn't be very expensive.

Dining Room

There are many ideas for using antiques in your dining room. Since few of us are fortunate enough to enjoy maids and gracious living, we no longer use such items as plated egg sets, cake baskets, cruets with bottles in plated mounts, asparagus servers, and so forth. However, with a little ingenuity, we can still have luxurious meals every so often.

If you don't care to serve boiled eggs in an ornate stand, why not use the stand as a cruet? Or bring an epergne to life by filling it with flowers. Single lusters—those vases with cut glass drops hanging around—usually can be bought at a reasonable price because of the traditional insistence on pairs. One with some trailing flowers in the top could look lovely.

Because glass, even good cut glass, is so difficult to display well in a shop or stall, it tends to be cheap, so it would be possible to adorn a dining table with glass at a reasonable cost. Colored glass will never be cheap, but just one piece could give a table a lift.

Double wooden tea caddies in a rectangular box shape, are also slow sellers and usually cheap. But often they are beautifully made of lovely wood; they could hold sugar, or candy, or cigarettes on a table.

Sitting Room

This room is probably too conservative for much experimentation, although there are possibilities for unusual furnishings that don't look out of place. Wastepaper baskets and log baskets need not be traditional containers, but could be something more exotic. A collection of small objects, such as perfume bottles, could be displayed under a glass-topped coffee table. Very few people have the courage to buy one really good antique and display it as a central feature—they feel happier with a lot of small pieces.

Lamps

There couldn't be a better way of furnishing a home with antiques than by using old lamps or making lamp conversions, but I think people are less imaginative than they might be. Admittedly, it's not so easy as it looks to convert oil lamps or anything else to safe electric lamps, but, considering the price of new ones, I think it's well worth the effort.

The simplest way is to buy one of those plastic lamp fitments with an adjustable piece at the bottom to fit into a variety of neck apertures, and a flex that comes straight out from the fitment so that it doesn't need to be taken through the bottom of the lamp. These fitments are all right as long as the lamp is reasonably wide and has its back to the wall to hide the flex, but otherwise it will look rather ugly.

Boring a hole through an old oil lamp is not necessarily a straightforward operation. There are some problems: drilling the glass container can sometimes take up to two days, because it often has a long solid piece of glass at the bottom to hold it in the metal part; carriage lamps sometimes have springs or old mending solder inside them, which have to be circumnavigated; and at any stage an unexpected obstruction may be encountered. So be prepared for a conversion to cost more than you might expect.

Few people explore the possibilities of turning broken vases into lamps, although sometimes the results can be gorgeous. If the top rim is chipped, a glass grinder will smooth it down. Then drill a hole in the bottom, fill the interior with sawdust to keep the lamp stable, make a wooden holder for the top to hold the electric fitment—and you may, with minimum cost and effort, end up with a superior piece of furnishing. To make the lamp look even better, put the vase on one of those carved Oriental wood stands, which may be bought in modern import shops.

Candlesticks, especially single ones which can often be bought quite cheaply, offer similar possibilities; however, the wire needs to go right through to make a neat job, and not many candlesticks are hollow.

Miscellaneous

An increasing number of people are realizing that Victorian pull front coal boxes, full-size ones resembling little tables, make marvelous and cheap telephone tables.

Victorian tapestries often turn up either in heavy frames or in rather ugly firescreens; it is quite easy to use the tapestry to make an original cushion.

Brass mortars without their pestles are often to be found quite cheaply; they make handy containers for pens and pencils.

19 List of Suppliers

Barometer repairs and parts.

Charles W. Mayher and Sons
5 South Wabash Avenue
Chicago, Illinois

Marshall Field and Company
111 North State Street
Chicago, Illinois

Book cleaner and dressing.

Marshall Field and Company
111 North State Street
Chicago, Illinois

Carpet cleaner and stain remover.

Marshall Field and Company
111 North State Street
Chicago, Illinois

Carson Pirie Scott and Company
1 South State Street
Chicago, Illinois

Chemicals.

Chemicals mentioned in the text can be purchased at most drugstores, especially Walgreen's Drugs. Specific chemicals are usually sold only in large quantities. Some chemical products may be secured also in hardware stores.

Clock repairs and parts.

Chicago Clock Company
22 West Madison Street
Chicago, Illinois

Doll supplies (clothing, wigs, shoes, accessories).

Antique Doll Hospital
3104 West Irving Park Road
Chicago, Illinois

Fabric, dolls'.

G. Fishman's and Sons, Inc.
1101 South Desplaines Street
Chicago, Illinois

Marshall Field and Company
111 North State Street
Chicago, Illinois

Fabric, upholstery.

Carson Pirie Scott and Company
1 South State Street
Chicago, Illinois

England Upholstery
    Manufacturing Company
666 North Lake Shore Drive
Chicago, Illinois

Home Fabrics
3350 North Paulina Street
Chicago, Illinois

Marshall Field and Company
111 North State Street
Chicago, Illinois

Furniture polish and cleaner.

Herbert Stanley Company
(manufacturer of Weiman's
products)
8140 Ridgeway
Skokie, Illinois

Furniture springs.

Nachman Corporation
4560 West Armitage Avenue
Chicago, Illinois

Marble cleaner and polish.

Herbert Stanley Company
(manufacturer of Weiman's
products)
8140 Ridgeway
Skokie, Illinois

Marshall Field and Company
111 North State Street
Chicago, Illinois

Silver (assaying, cleaning, plating, refining).

House of Williams
37 South Wabash Avenue
Chicago, Illinois

Index